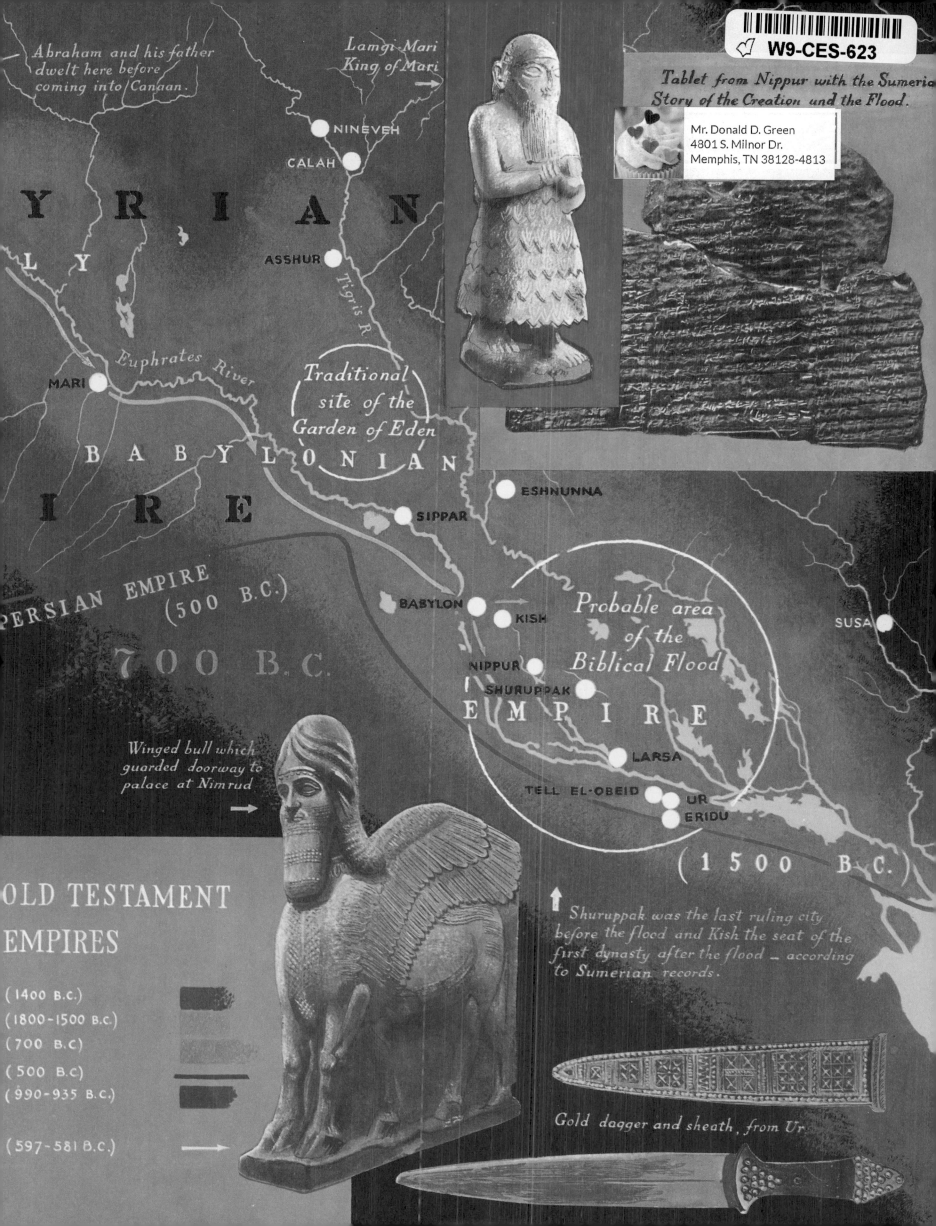

Abraham and his father dwelt here before coming into Canaan.

Lamgi-Mari King of Mari

Tablet from Nippur with the Sumerian Story of the Creation and the Flood.

NINEVEH
CALAH
ASSHUR

Tigris R.

Euphrates River

MARI

Traditional site of the Garden of Eden

BABYLONIAN

EMPIRE

ESHNUNNA
SIPPAR

PERSIAN EMPIRE (500 B.C.)

700 B.C.

BABYLON
KISH
Probable area of the Biblical Flood
SUSA

NIPPUR
SHURUPPAK

EMPIRE

Winged bull which guarded doorway to palace at Nimrud

LARSA

TELL EL-OBEID
UR
ERIDU

(1500 B.C.)

Shuruppak was the last ruling city before the flood and Kish the seat of the first dynasty after the flood — according to Sumerian records.

OLD TESTAMENT
EMPIRES

(1400 B.C.)
(1800-1500 B.C.)
(700 B.C.)
(500 B.C.)
(990-935 B.C.)

(597-581 B.C.)

Gold dagger and sheath, from Ur

THE GOLDEN
BIBLE ATLAS

BY **SAMUEL** TERRIEN

DAVENPORT PROFESSOR OF HEBREW AND THE COGNATE LANGUAGES
UNION THEOLOGICAL SEMINARY AND COLUMBIA UNIVERSITY

ILLUSTRATED BY **WILLIAM** BOLIN

gb **GOLDEN** PRESS **NEW** YORK

Western Publishing Company, Inc.
Racine, Wisconsin

CONTENTS

The lands in which the people of the Bible moved occupy only a small area of the world.

ACKNOWLEDGMENTS

BLACK AND WHITE PHOTOGRAPHS—P. 15 (top) Baghdad milking scene, (bottom) Frieze of bulls, *University Museum of the University of Pennsylvania.* P. 18 Great Sphinx of Gizeh, *TWA, Inc.* P. 20 (top) Amenhotep, *Egyptian Exploration Society,* (bottom) Hieroglyphic, *Metropolitan Museum of Art.* P. 24 (top) Monastery, (bottom) Wilderness of Sinai, *Max G. Scheler, Magnum Photos, Inc.* P. 34 Mizpah, *Matson Photo Service, Los Angeles.* P. 36 The Rock Moriah from the Dome, *Matson Photo Service, Los Angeles.* P. 38 Walls of Jerusalem, *Fritz Henle, Monkmeyer Press Photo Service.* P. 43 Cedars of Lebanon, *University Museum of the University of Pennsylvania.* P. 46 Megiddo ivories, *Oriental Institute, University of Chicago.* P. 49 (top) Tiglath-pileser III, (bottom) Ashurnasirpal hunting lion, *British Museum.* P. 54 Apadana at Persepolis, *Oriental Institute, University of Chicago.* P. 56 Persepolis, Lion attacking bull, *Oriental Institute, University of Chicago.* P. 61 Cleopatra, *Archives Photographiques, Paris.* P. 62 Roman ruins, *Scofield, Ewing Galloway, New York.* P. 63 Hills of Judea, *George Rodger, Magnum Photos, Inc.* P. 64 Mary's Well, *Eastman Collection.* P. 68 Jacob's Well, *Matson Photo service, Los Angeles.* P. 70-71 Jerusalem from Mount of Olives, *George Rodger, Magnum Photos, Inc.* P. 72 Via Dolorosa, *Eastman Collec-*

tion. P. 73 Garden of Gethsemane, *George Rodger, Magnum Photos, Inc.* P. 75 Garden tomb, Jerusalem, *TWA, Inc.* P. 83 The Appian Way, *TWA, Inc.*

COLOR PHOTOS—P. 6 Sunrise over Judea, *Inge Morath, Magnum Photos, Inc.* P. 16 Jordan River, *Inge Morath, Magnum.* P. 17 Mosque of Machpellah, *Three Lions.* P. 18 Tut-ankh-amen, *Paul Scherer.* P. 43 Solomon's Pool, *Paul Scherer.* P. 46 Omri's Walls, *Paul Scherer.* P. 50 Spring of Gihon, *Paul Scherer.* P. 64 Nazareth, *Three Lions.* P. 66 Mt. of Temptation, *Inge Morath, Magnum Photos, Inc.* P. 67 (top) Sea of Galilee, (bottom) Capernaum, *Three Lions.* P. 76 Gate called "Beautiful," *Three Lions.* P. 79 Parthenon, *John Moore.* P. 90 Mosque of Omar, *Three Lions.* P. 92 (top) Reforestation on the road to Jerusalem, (bottom) Dam, Israel, *David Seymour, Magnum Photos, Inc.*

ILLUSTRATIONS—P. 41 Megiddo stables, based on model by *Oriental Institute, University of Chicago.* P. 47 Sargon, based on restoration of *Oriental Institute, University of Chicago.* P. 74-75 Garden tomb, modification of illustration in *Nelson's Atlas of the Bible.*

FOREWORD

Asiatics from an Egyptian wall painting

MANY PEOPLE think of the Bible as a collection of separate stories. Actually the Bible is all one story, whether we stop with the Old Testament or go on through the New Testament.

For the Bible has one main purpose, even though it was written slowly, over hundreds of years, by many different persons. That purpose is to show how God's plan for saving mankind was worked out through the ages, in the daily lives of men and women. The history of the ancient Hebrews and of the early Christians thus becomes the story of God's love for the world, and of man's search for the true meaning of life.

The men and women of the Bible had the same needs and feelings that people have today. They knew hunger and thirst, fear and pain. They were sometimes happy and sometimes sad. Some of them were heroes, and some of them were cowards. They had to choose between good and evil, and the choice was just as hard for them as it is for us. They were real people with real problems.

The world in which they lived was, of course, different from ours. To understand how they felt and why they behaved as they did, we must first understand their land.

The land of the Bible is a varied one. It has hot, dry deserts, mountains both barren and fertile, and green river valleys. The deserts have just enough water to grow grass here and there. People can live in the deserts, but they must move about to find enough pasture for their sheep and goats. In the river valleys, on the other hand, the soil is rich and grows grain and fruit. Most of southern Palestine is barren mountains and desert. The north, with its valleys and green mountain slopes, is rather fertile.

The story of the Bible takes place in the deserts, on mountain slopes, and in the valleys. The people of the deserts were nomads who wandered about with their flocks. The people of the river valleys and fertile mountain slopes were farmers who settled down to cultivate the land. The nomads and the farmers did not understand each other, and fighting often broke out between them.

The Bible becomes clear and vivid to us if we read it with maps and pictures at hand. This book has two purposes: to show the land that shaped the people, and to depict the people's story against the background of their land. The maps and pictures thus follow the Old and the New Testaments in the order of the story which they tell.

To read the Bible from Genesis to Revelation is to make a long journey in space and time. Setting out from Ur in Mesopotamia, we pass through Palestine into Egypt, then out of Egypt into the wilderness and the Promised Land. We go from Jerusalem to Babylon, to Antioch, and to Rome—and even to the "new Jerusalem" at the end of time.

And, as we move through the land of the Bible, and watch the drama that took place there long ago, we hear again the word of a God who now, as always, stands above our world and our lives.

Samuel Terrien

9

THE BEGINNINGS

Genesis, Chapters 1 to 11

THE WORLD of the Bible was not large. It included only southwestern Asia and the northeastern part of Africa. This whole area is about as big as the southeastern corner of the United States—from Maryland to Florida and from the Atlantic to the Mississippi.

Only a small part of these regions can be cultivated. Much of the area is mountain and desert. The only fertile parts are the river valleys.

The whole land of Egypt, for instance, is just a narrow green ribbon along the River Nile. This thin strip of fields and gardens is hemmed in on both sides by high cliffs of pink granite or slopes of sand and pebbles.

Along the Tigris and Euphrates Rivers to the east is another green strip which was once called Mesopotamia—a name which means "The Land between the Two Rivers." In Bible times Mesopotamia was a long and in places broad band of fertile ground, bordered on one side by the mountains of Persia and on the other by the desert of Arabia. The line of separation between the fruitful soil and the desert hills was so clear that a man could walk in a single step from the black, living earth of the valley to the dry, dead sand of the surrounding slopes.

The invention of the plow marked the beginning of settled civilization; it allowed man to till the soil and grow his food instead of wandering in search of it.

THE BEGINNINGS OF CIVILIZATION

It was in the green strips of Mesopotamia and Egypt that civilization began. Perhaps as early as 4500 B.C. the settlers started to build dikes, and to dig irrigation ditches and drainage canals.

In these valleys, the water of the rivers made the soil extremely rich, but also marshy. The rivers flooded every year and often changed course, leaving vast swamps. To be able to live in the valleys, the inhabitants had to build walls

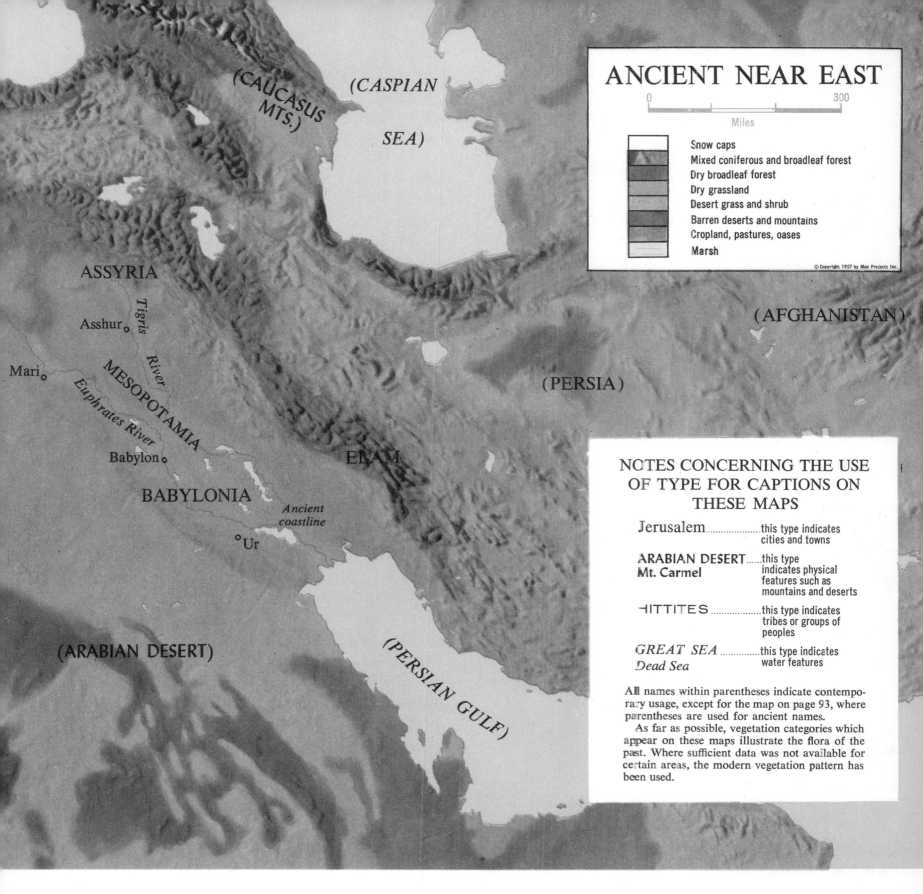

ANCIENT NEAR EAST

0   300
Miles

- Snow caps
- Mixed coniferous and broadleaf forest
- Dry broadleaf forest
- Dry grassland
- Desert grass and shrub
- Barren deserts and mountains
- Cropland, pastures, oases
- Marsh

© Copyright 1957 by Map Projects Inc.

(CAUCASUS MTS.)

(CASPIAN SEA)

ASSYRIA

Asshur

Tigris River

Mari

MESOPOTAMIA

Euphrates River

Babylon

BABYLONIA

Ancient coastline

Ur

ELAM

(AFGHANISTAN)

(PERSIA)

(ARABIAN DESERT)

(PERSIAN GULF)

NOTES CONCERNING THE USE OF TYPE FOR CAPTIONS ON THESE MAPS

Jerusalem ....this type indicates cities and towns

ARABIAN DESERT ......this type indicates physical
Mt. Carmel   features such as mountains and deserts

HITTITES ....this type indicates tribes or groups of peoples

GREAT SEA ....this type indicates
Dead Sea   water features

All names within parentheses indicate contemporary usage, except for the map on page 93, where parentheses are used for ancient names.

As far as possible, vegetation categories which appear on these maps illustrate the flora of the past. Where sufficient data was not available for certain areas, the modern vegetation pattern has been used.

to keep the flood waters back and drain the swamps by digging canals. No single family could do such jobs alone. Men of different families and clans had to learn how to work together to build the walls and dig the canals and keep them in repair. Engineers had to be trained who could plan how the ditches and walls should be built. This was one of the important ways in which human society with government and laws came into being.

The digging of the canals did three things: it drained the swamps, it controlled the floods, and it provided a network of waterways on which boats could carry men and goods. Long before there were land roads, canals offered a swift and smooth road by water. Harvests were so plentiful that the extra food could be exchanged for goods produced elsewhere—for spices, fragrant woods, jewels, and swords and spears of metal.

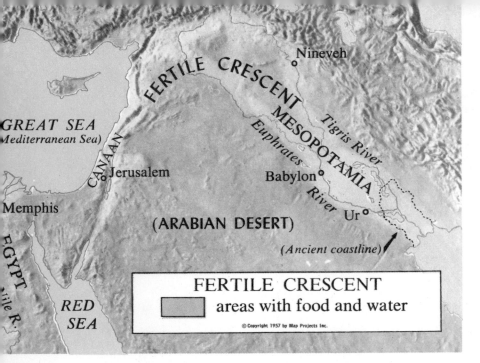

FERTILE CRESCENT
areas with food and water

© Copyright 1957 by Map Projects Inc.

As a result, the inhabitants of the river valleys became wealthy. This made them tempting prey to the poor and hungry nomads who lived in the desert hills. Mesopotamia, for example, was conquered again and again by invaders. Sometimes war and invasion left the flood walls and canals unrepaired too long. Then the valley would again become a swamp, until a new and strong ruler came along and got the irrigation system back in operation.

THE FERTILE CRESCENT

Gradually the rulers of both Mesopotamia and Egypt grew more powerful; they began to reach out toward each other in both peace and war. But travelers and armies could not cross the almost waterless Arabian desert. They had to make their way through the green fingers of the valleys in Syria, and along the coastal plain of Palestine at the eastern end of the Mediterranean. Even before the dawn of written history, Palestine became the land bridge between Mesopotamia and Egypt, and the crossroads of the ancient world.

Because the soil here was richer than that of the surrounding areas, this region is often called the Fertile Crescent. The peoples who lived in Palestine and Syria came into contact with the customs and ideas of Mesopotamia and Egypt.

It is not surprising to find echoes of Mesopotamia in the Bible. The Hebrews may have remembered life in the marshy plains of lower Mesopotamia when they described the creation of the world: "And God said, 'Let the waters . . . be gathered together in one place, and let the dry land appear!' "

THE TRADITION OF THE FLOOD

In Mesopotamia, also, there was a tradition of a Great Flood, and a story about a man who survived it, named Ut-napishtim. According to the story, an angry god decided to destroy the world, but another god, friendly to man, told Ut-napishtim to build a great ship and take his family on board. Ut-napishtim obeyed; in a fearful storm, the waters rose and drowned all human beings except those on the ship. After many days, Ut-napishtim sent out birds to search for dry land. Finally the ship was grounded on a mountain top. There Ut-napishtim offered sacrifices, and the gods, who were hungry for the smell of roasted meat, promised him that they would not send a flood on the earth again.

In many ways, the story of Ut-napishtim is like the story of Noah. In the Mesopotamian story, however, the gods behave like quarreling

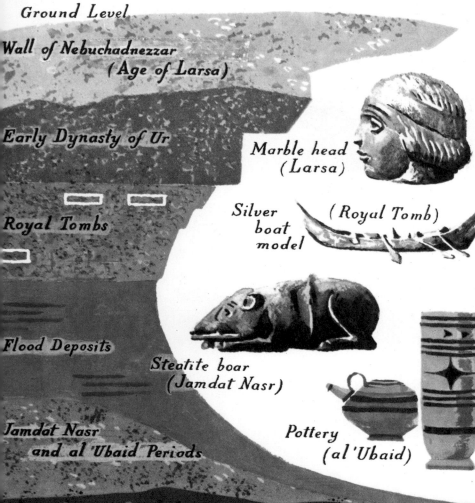

Ground Level

Wall of Nebuchadnezzar
(Age of Larsa)

Early Dynasty of Ur

Marble head
(Larsa)

Silver boat model   (Royal Tomb)

Royal Tombs

Steatite boar
(Jamdat Nasr)

Flood Deposits

Jamdat Nasr
and al 'Ubaid Periods

Pottery
(al 'Ubaid)

Original Island

Archaeologists—men who study the past by digging out ancient ruins and examining them—have found that there once really was a great flood in Mesopotamia. The flood left massive layers of mud and clay, which meant it must have been terribly destructive. Here is a cross section of the diggings at Ur and some of the objects found.

children, but in the Bible, God is just. He destroys men in the Flood because they have grown impossibly wicked; but Noah, as an honest man, is saved to begin the human race over again.

THE STORY OF THE TOWER OF BABEL

Another echo of Mesopotamia is found in the story of the Tower of Babel. The Sumerians, an early people who lived in the lower Euphrates valley, and the Babylonians, who lived there later, were both in the habit of building high towers called *ziggurats*. A ziggurat was usually a square or rectangular pile of clay bricks, seven stories high. A ramp or staircase wound around it on the outside, from the ground to the top.

The Babylonians used ziggurats in their religious ceremonies. In the Book of Genesis, however, the Tower of Babel is a symbol of man's desire to become God's equal.

The Hebrews seem to have taken some of their earliest stories from the legends of the ancient world. However, they rewrote these stories, and

The ziggurat of Ur was 200 feet long and 150 feet wide. It rose about 70 feet from the flat plain, and its terraces were probably planted with trees and shrubs. Its ruins still stand.

changed them in many ways. These stories are no longer legends or myths about storms and earthquakes and other fearful aspects of nature. They become parts of the drama of mankind.

The great theme of Genesis is the history of God's relations with men. From the story of the creation to the story of the Tower of Babel, the book tries to show that men become lost and miserable when they forget God. Then, with the calling of Abraham, the Bible begins the long account of God's attempts to save men from destruction and death.

According to the Bible, Noah's sons—Ham, Shem, and Japheth— left the ark to father the peoples of the world.

THE PATRIARCHAL AGE

ABOUT 2000–1400 B.C.

Genesis, Chapters 12 to 50

Babylonian picture of the universe

ABRAHAM, Isaac, Jacob, and Joseph—these were the Patriarchs, the great founding fathers of the Hebrew nation. For centuries, their names and deeds were recited around the campfires of the Fertile Crescent. Men sang the tales to their sons, who, in turn, sang them to their sons. The tradition was carried in this manner.

Only after hundreds of years were the tales written down in a connected story. The purpose of this story, as the Bible tells it, is to show that Hebrew history has a meaning for the whole human race. God promised Abraham that his children's children would some day live at peace with "all the families of the earth."

THE HOME OF ABRAHAM

Abraham's father is thought to have come from Ur of the Chaldeans, an ancient city in southern Mesopotamia. Abraham lived in Haran, several hundred miles northwest of Ur.

Probably Abraham's people were Amorites. The Amorites had invaded Mesopotamia from the Arabian desert, about the nineteenth century B.C. They conquered the Sumerians who then lived in the southern part of the Euphrates valley. Taking over much of the Sumerians' culture, science, and religion, the Amorites built a mighty kingdom with the city of Babylon as its capital. This kingdom was known as the First Babylonian Empire.

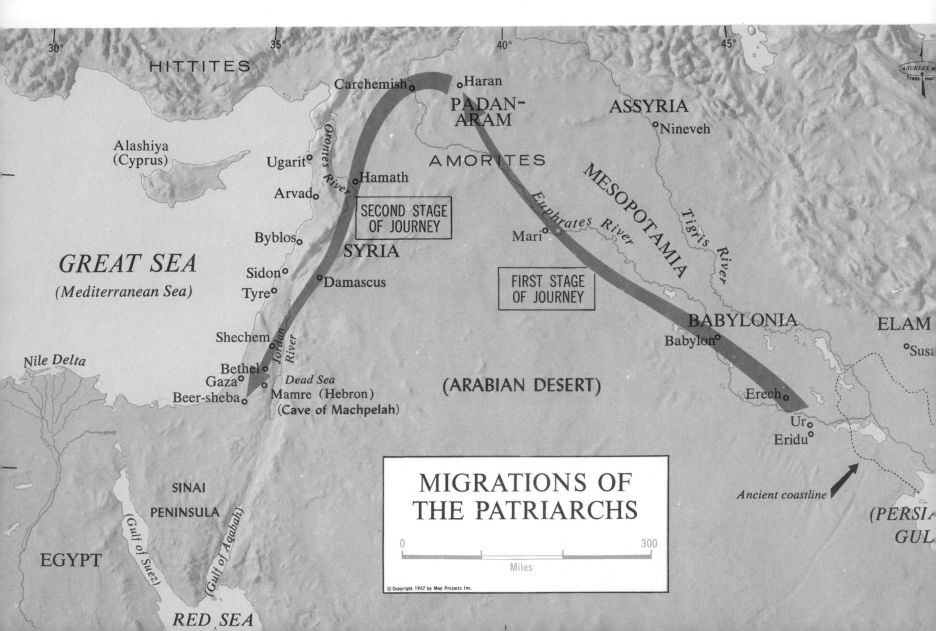

HITTITES

Carchemish

Haran

PADAN-ARAM

ASSYRIA

Nineveh

Alashiya (Cyprus)

Ugarit

AMORITES

MESOPOTAMIA

Tigris River

Hamath

Arvad

Orontes River

SECOND STAGE OF JOURNEY

Byblos

SYRIA

Euphrates River

Mari

FIRST STAGE OF JOURNEY

GREAT SEA
(Mediterranean Sea)

Sidon

Tyre

Damascus

BABYLONIA

ELAM

Babylon

Susa

Shechem

Jordan River

Bethel

Gaza

Dead Sea

Mamre (Hebron)
(Cave of Machpelah)

(ARABIAN DESERT)

Beer-sheba

Erech

Ur

Eridu

SINAI PENINSULA

(Gulf of Aqabah)

(Gulf of Suez)

Ancient coastline

(PERSIAN GULF)

EGYPT

Nile Delta

SUREAX Trade mar

MIGRATIONS OF THE PATRIARCHS

0   300

Miles

© Copyright 1957 by Map Projects Inc.

RED SEA

Mesopotamians making butter, from the time of Abraham.

The people of Babylon worshiped the stars and the planets, and especially the sun and the moon. In both Ur and Haran there were temples dedicated to the moon-god. Legends say that Abraham left his father's house because he would not worship his father's idols.

FROM HARAN TO CANAAN

Abraham left the city of Haran and a land of plenty behind him in obedience to God's command. He became a nomad, making a hard living in the desert with his flocks. Abraham moved along slowly with his clan and his animals, from one well or spring to the next. He traveled westward and then southward along the edge of the Fertile Crescent to the land of Canaan.

A narrow band of plains, valleys, and mountains, Canaan was about the size of the present state of Massachusetts. It stretched one hundred and fifty miles from Mount Hermon in the north to the Negeb in the south, and fifty miles from the Mediterranean Sea to the deep canyon of the Jordan River and the Dead Sea. The Canaanites were cousins of the Phoenicians, who lived farther north along the Mediterranean coast.

Since the Phoenicians had good harbors, they were traders and sailors. South of Mount Carmel, however, there were no sheltered places for ships. So the Canaanites became farmers, smiths, and merchants. They lived inside walled cities, but went outside the walls to cultivate their fields.

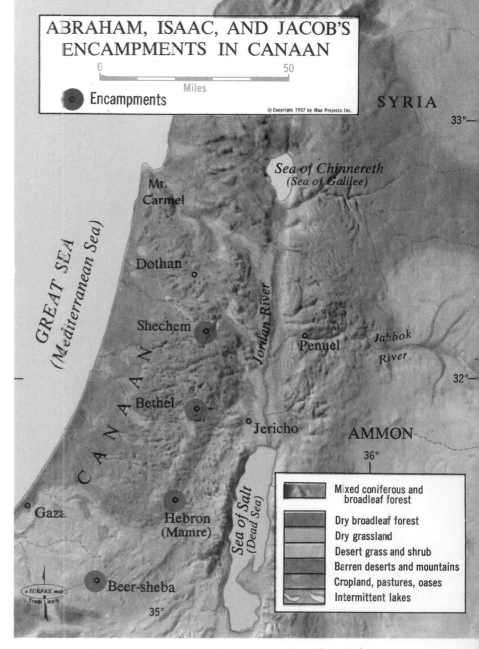

ABRAHAM, ISAAC, AND JACOB'S ENCAMPMENTS IN CANAAN

0   50

Miles

● Encampments

© Copyright 1957 by Map Projects Inc.

SYRIA

Sea of Chinnereth (Sea of Galilee)

Mt. Carmel

GREAT SEA (Mediterranean Sea)

Dothan

Jordan River

Shechem

Penuel

Jabbok River

C A N A A N

Bethel

Jericho

AMMON

Gaza

Hebron (Mamre)

Sea of Salt (Dead Sea)

Beer-sheba

a SURFAX map Trade mark

	Mixed coniferous and broadleaf forest
	Dry broadleaf forest
	Dry grassland
	Desert grass and shrub
	Barren deserts and mountains
	Cropland, pastures, oases
	Intermittent lakes

A frieze of bulls, made of shell and laid in bitumen, from an early temple found near Ur.

The River Jordan flows through the deepest valley in the world. From its source in the snow-clad Anti-Lebanon Mountains of Syria, it twists over 200 miles to the Dead Sea, 1,200 feet below sea level. The Jordan is now used for irrigation.

Abraham built an altar to God at Shechem, another near Bethel, and a third at Mamre, near Hebron. Except for a hasty trip to Egypt to buy food during a famine, he seems to have moved around between one and another of these three places.

As the flocks and followers of Abraham and Lot became numerous, their servants began to argue over water for the animals.

Abraham and Lot talked the situation over and agreed to part. Abraham decided to stay in the mountains, with their stony soil and uncertain grass. Lot chose to move down into the fertile valley near the Dead Sea, to the "cities of the plain."

It is hard to imagine two places more unlike each other than the mountains of Canaan and the valley leading to the Dead Sea. From high ranges and hills, twenty-four hundred feet above sea level, the land drops swiftly down to the lowest spot on earth. There, twelve hundred feet below sea level, flowers bloom even in January, and birds sing in the warm sun. Properly irrigated, the fields grow several harvests a year.

Abraham's nomad way of life kept him and his tribe apart from the Canaanites. When he died, he was buried in the cave of Machpelah near Mamre.

ISAAC IN THE NEGEB

Like his father Abraham, Isaac moved about with his flocks and did not mingle with the Canaanites. When the time came for Isaac to marry, Abraham sent all the way back to Haran, in Mesopotamia, to find a wife for him. This was Rebekah, the daughter of one of Abraham's own kinsmen.

Isaac and his family moved back and forth between Canaan and the region known as the Negeb. In this land of dry sand hills and rocky plateaus, every drop of water was carefully hoarded. Cisterns were cut in the rock, and small

The land of Canaan had no central government. Practically every walled city had its king, who ruled the land around it and spent much time fighting the other kings. The Pharaohs (Kings) of Egypt were supposed to rule over these petty kings, but Egypt was far away. The Canaanite kings wrote letters to their Egyptian rulers. Some of these letters, found in Tell-el-Amarna in Egypt, complain about the *Habiru*, nomads from the eastern desert who came in to raid the rich Canaanite harvests. Some of these "Habiru" may have been the "Hebrews."

THE MOUNTAIN AND THE VALLEY

Abraham did not set out for the land of Canaan alone. His nephew Lot came with him. Each man had a family, servants, and animals.

16

Abraham and his family, servants, and animals moved through the Fertile Crescent, encamping near water points.

gutters were dug to keep the rain water in them. Owning cisterns and wells was a matter of life and death. In the valley of Gerar, Isaac's shepherds quarreled with other shepherds over certain wells, and Isaac moved on to Beer-sheba, the "well of the seven." When Isaac died, he was buried in the cave of Machpelah, beside his father Abraham.

THE TRAVELS OF JACOB

Isaac had two sons, Esau and Jacob. After tricking Esau out of his inheritance, Jacob had to run away from his brother's anger. He, too, went back to Haran to find a wife. On the way he stopped at his grandfather Abraham's altar at Bethel, and it was there he had a vision of the heavenly ladder.

At Haran, Jacob married the sisters Leah and Rachel, from among his mother's kinsfolk. Returning to Canaan years later, with his wives and children and many animals and servants, he began to worry about meeting his brother Esau, whose anger he still feared.

One night, he sent his company on ahead and stayed by himself, down in the deep, narrow canyon of the Jabbok. There, says the Bible, he wrestled all night with an unknown being, who made him lame and also gave him a new name. Instead of Jacob, or "kicker," he became Israel, "God fights."

Finally, Jacob and Esau did meet, and the old quarrel was healed. Jacob—or Israel—became the ancestor of the Israelites, and Esau the ancestor of the Edomites.

JOSEPH IN EGYPT

When Jacob sent Joseph, his son by Rachel, to visit his other sons at Dothan, they seized the young man and sold him to a passing caravan of Midianites or Ishmaelites. The caravan took Joseph to Egypt and sold him in Egypt as a slave.

Joseph rose to be the prime minister of the Pharaoh himself. When famine in Canaan drove Joseph's brothers down into Egypt to buy food, Joseph was able to help them. He sent for the aged Israel, his father, and settled all the family there. Thus began the long stay of the Hebrews in the land of Egypt.

This mosque at Hebron covers the patriarchs' tomb in the cave of Machpelah, the first plot of land owned by the Hebrews in Canaan.

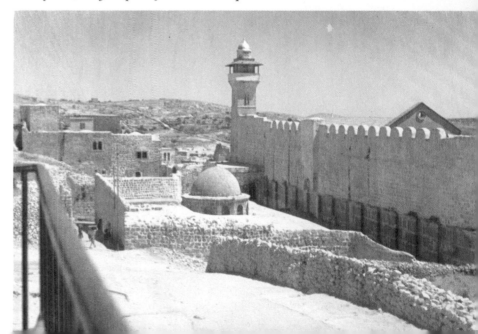

Gold mask of
Tutankhamen

THE EGYPTIAN EMPIRE
AND THE EXODUS

ABOUT 1275 B.C.

Exodus, Chapters 1 to 15

AT THE southwestern tip of the Fertile Crescent lies the land of Egypt. On the map it looks like a big country, covering the northeastern corner of Africa; but most of the land is a desert. The only livable part of Egypt is the fifteen-hundred-mile-long green valley of the River Nile.

THE LIFE-GIVING NILE

During the summer, the rivers of the Near East dry up or shrink to mere trickles. But not the River Nile. Every July and August, far in the south at the equator, heavy rains feed the river's sources. Soon a mighty flood covers the Nile valley and the lowland of the river delta.

The flood reaches its highest point in September or October. Then, as the river slowly withdraws to its bed, it leaves a layer of mud which enriches the soil.

Through the winter and spring seasons, the irrigated fields, gardens, and orchards grow huge crops of cereals and fruits. Canals are full of fish. The marshes bloom with lotus flowers and are green with papyrus, a reed from which a paper-like sheet can be prepared for writing.

The fruitful soil and mild climate of the Nile

The Sphinx at Gizeh, on the edge of the Nile valley, is carved from a natural stone mass. In it is a temple.

The Nile valley was alive with birds and animals—gazelles, antelopes, lions, panthers, hippopotamuses, and crocodiles.

valley made it the home of one of man's earliest civilizations. Over five thousand years ago, the people who lived there had a prosperous and settled society. In the Early Kingdom or Pyramid Age (about 3000–2700 B.C.), the Pharaohs built a vast empire. During the Middle Kingdom (about 2000–1800 B.C.), Egypt controlled a large part of the Fertile Crescent. Then Egypt was conquered by invaders from Asia; but by 1546 B.C. it entered the period of its greatest glory and wealth—the New Kingdom, which lasted several hundred years.

EGYPTIAN CIVILIZATION

For centuries, the Pharaohs built magnificent temples, palaces, and cities along the Nile. In the temples of Karnak, near Luxor, the traveler of today is still awed by the forests of gigantic columns and the carvings on the walls.

In the Valley of the Kings, the embalmed mummies of the Pharaohs were buried in small tombs carved in the rock, with royal furniture, supplies of food, and immense treasures. Most of these tombs were robbed centuries ago. In modern times, however, the tomb of young King Tutankhamen was discovered almost untouched. The treasures from this one tomb fill several large halls in the Cairo Museum.

The ancient Egyptians were not only great architects, sculptors, and painters; they were also poets, writers, scientists, and mathematicians. Many of their "books" survive—engraved in gran-

ite, painted on the walls of tombs, or written on fragile sheets of papyrus. The scribes—who wrote the picture-language or hieroglyphics—together with the priests and the military officers formed the privileged classes of Egyptian society.

Ordinary men and women led hard lives. The building of pyramids, palaces, and temples, the work of keeping up the canals, dikes, and irrigation ditches—all these required thousands of slaves. The civilization of Egypt was paid for with human blood and social injustices.

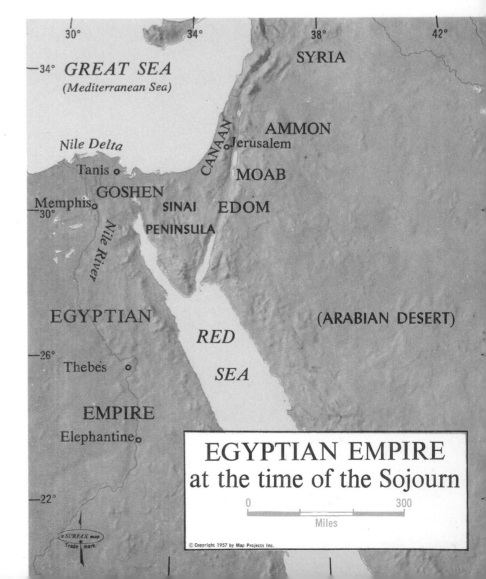

EGYPTIAN EMPIRE
at the time of the Sojourn

0   300
Miles

© Copyright 1957 by Map Projects Inc.

The pictures at left and center of a modern Egyptian show the facial characteristics of Amenophis IV on the right.

EGYPTIAN RELIGION

Both the common people and the ruling classes were extremely religious. Like the Sumerians and the Babylonians, the ancient Egyptians worshiped a great array of gods and goddesses, with elaborate ceremonies.

During the sojourn of the Hebrews in Egypt, a Pharaoh named Amenophis IV (1370–1353 B.C.) attempted a religious reform. He wanted to worship only Aton the sun god, maker of the earth and of all living things. To show his reverence to Aton, the Pharaoh even changed his own name to Ikhnaton.

THE OPPRESSION OF THE HEBREWS

The sons of Jacob settled in the eastern part of the Nile Delta (the "land of Goshen") during the time of Joseph. They were among the many nomads who had come to Egypt because of famine and had settled there.

For a while, the Hebrews prospered. Then a new Pharaoh rose to power, who "knew not Joseph" and was no longer kind to these strangers. He probably was Seti I (1319–1301 B.C.). Desiring to fortify the northeastern border of Egypt against invaders from Asia, he pressed the population of Goshen into slavery.

During Seti's reign and that of his successor, Ramses II, the Hebrews toiled to build the fortress of Pithom (near Lake Timsah) and to restore the city of Tanis as the new capital of the Egyptian empire.

Moses was brought up in the wealth and culture of Egypt. Nevertheless, he chose to side with his fellow Hebrews, and create a nation out of a mass of slaves. In the name of the Lord, he led his people out of the Pharaoh's reach. The memory of that heroic escape from Egypt, the "Exodus," remains the inspiration of Israel.

THE EXODUS

Moses did not lead the Hebrews out of Egypt by the direct highroad to the northeast, on which the Egyptian soldiers could easily have

A scribe to the queen, holding his tablet of hieroglyphics. This was the form of writing used in ancient Egypt.

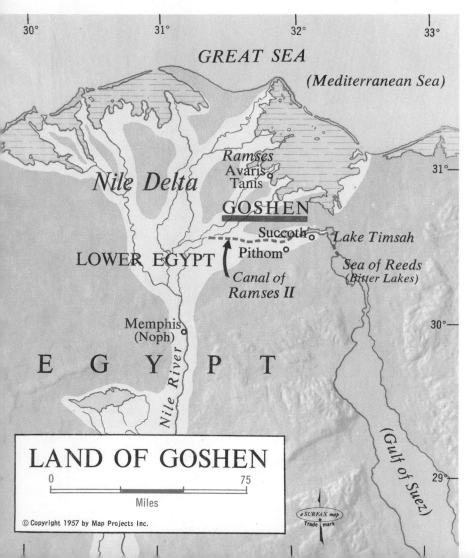

GREAT SEA
(Mediterranean Sea)

Ramses
Avaris
Tanis

Nile Delta

GOSHEN

Succoth
Lake Timsah

LOWER EGYPT
Pithom

Sea of Reeds
(Bitter Lakes)

Canal of
Ramses II

Memphis
(Noph)

E G Y P T

Nile River

(Gulf of Suez)

LAND OF GOSHEN

0 — 75

Miles

© Copyright 1957 by Map Projects Inc.

Pharaoh Ramses II offering a tribute to the gods.

Just as the fleeing Hebrews were reaching safety on the eastern shore, the Egyptians came to the western bank. There, the horsemen and their war chariots hurled themselves across the treacherous passage—only to bog down in the sand and drown in the returning waters.

The Hebrews felt then that their God, without temples or priests, was indeed more powerful than all the gods of Egypt and the most mighty army on earth. The next forty years were to be a long, hard test of their faith.

overtaken them. Instead, setting out from Succoth, halfway between Pithom and Lake Timsah, the Hebrews moved toward the marshes and the treacherous sands of the Sea of Reeds. They encamped, the first night, on its western banks. The Bible says that the place was Etham, not far from Pihahiroth, "between Migdol and the sea, before Baal-zephon." Unfortunately, the exact location of these sites is not known.

That night, the Egyptians sent horsemen and armed chariots in pursuit. Caught between the rugged hills on the west and the Sea of Reeds, the Hebrews would have been trapped.

The level of water in the Bitter Lakes was higher in those days. A large region that is now dry was then covered with shallow water. The exact path followed by the Hebrews cannot be traced, but as the Bible puts it, "The Lord caused the sea to go back by a strong wind all the night, and made the sea dry land and the waters were divided."

The Egyptians were skilled jewelers, noted for their beautiful designs and use of gold and enamel. Here are ornaments from the New Egyptian Empire.

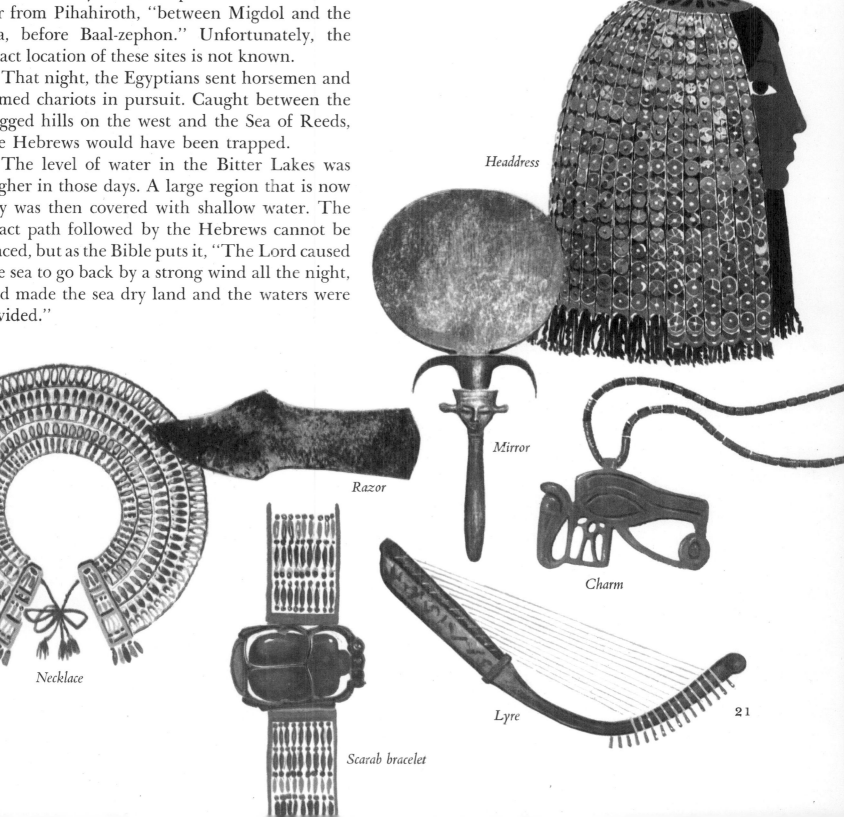

Headdress

Mirror

Razor

Charm

Necklace

Lyre

21

Scarab bracelet

The Ten Commandments

SINAI AND THE WANDERING IN THE WILDERNESS

ABOUT 1275–1235 B.C.

Exodus, Chapters 16 to 40; *Numbers, Deuteronomy*

FROM THE Sea of Reeds, Moses led the Hebrews onward into the "wilderness" (desert) of Shur. For three days the people marched and found no water. And when they came to Marah the water was too salty to drink. Marah (in Hebrew, "bitterness") is probably the present brackish spring of Ain Hawarah.

The next camping site was Elim (the modern Wadi Gharandel), with its twelve springs of water and seventy palm trees. Then the Hebrews reached the wilderness of Sin. With the cool sea breezes cut off by the hills, the sun beat down savagely on the rocky canyons, and the people began to grumble. They thought longingly of the "fleshpots" of Egypt, a land in which they at least had had enough to eat.

MOUNT SINAI

Pushing always east and south to the high mountain mass in the southern part of the Sinai Peninsula, the caravan reached Rephidim. There, in order to pass, the Hebrews had to fight some Amelek Bedouins. Next, they stopped for a while with friendly nomads of the clan of Midian. At last they arrived in the wilderness of Sinai at the foot of the Mountain of God.

We are not quite certain of the exact location of Mount Sinai (also called Mount Horeb). An Arab tradition going back to the fourth century A.D. names one of the peaks Djebel Musa, "The Mount of Moses." This may indeed be the Biblical Mount Sinai, because at its base is the only large spring of water in the region. The Hebrews could not have encamped so long near Sinai without an adequate water supply.

Moses knew this region well. Years before, he had tended sheep there for his father-in-law, and

had seen the vision of the burning bush. Now, climbing alone to the top of the peak, eight thousand feet above sea level, he met his God in the midst of thunders and lightnings and received the Ten Commandments. On Sinai, God bound himself in a solemn covenant ("testament") with the people of Israel, and the Israelites became aware of their mission in history as a "holy nation."

Even today, in the sunlight of a peaceful spring morning, the panorama from Djebel Musa is astounding. Range after range of rose and yellow granite extends toward the north; in the other three directions, the peaks drop sharply downward. Far to the south, the two gulfs—Suez in the west and Aqabah in the east—join and disappear in the heat haze of the Red Sea.

THE HEBREWS AT KADESH-BARNEA

Moses and his people remained at Sinai for about a year. Then they moved northward. Before them, several men carried the Ark of the Covenant. This was an empty chest of wood. It reminded them that God was always with them to guide and protect them, even though they could not see Him.

Passing through the desert of Paran, the Hebrews reached the tip of the Gulf of Aqabah, and then the oasis of Kadesh-barnea, about forty miles south of the Promised Land.

For thirty-eight long years, the weary Hebrews remained there. The men of the older generation, who had come out of Egypt, died one by one. But the life of the desert made their sons strong and hardy. As these grew to manhood, Moses and his lieutenant Joshua decided that it was time to act.

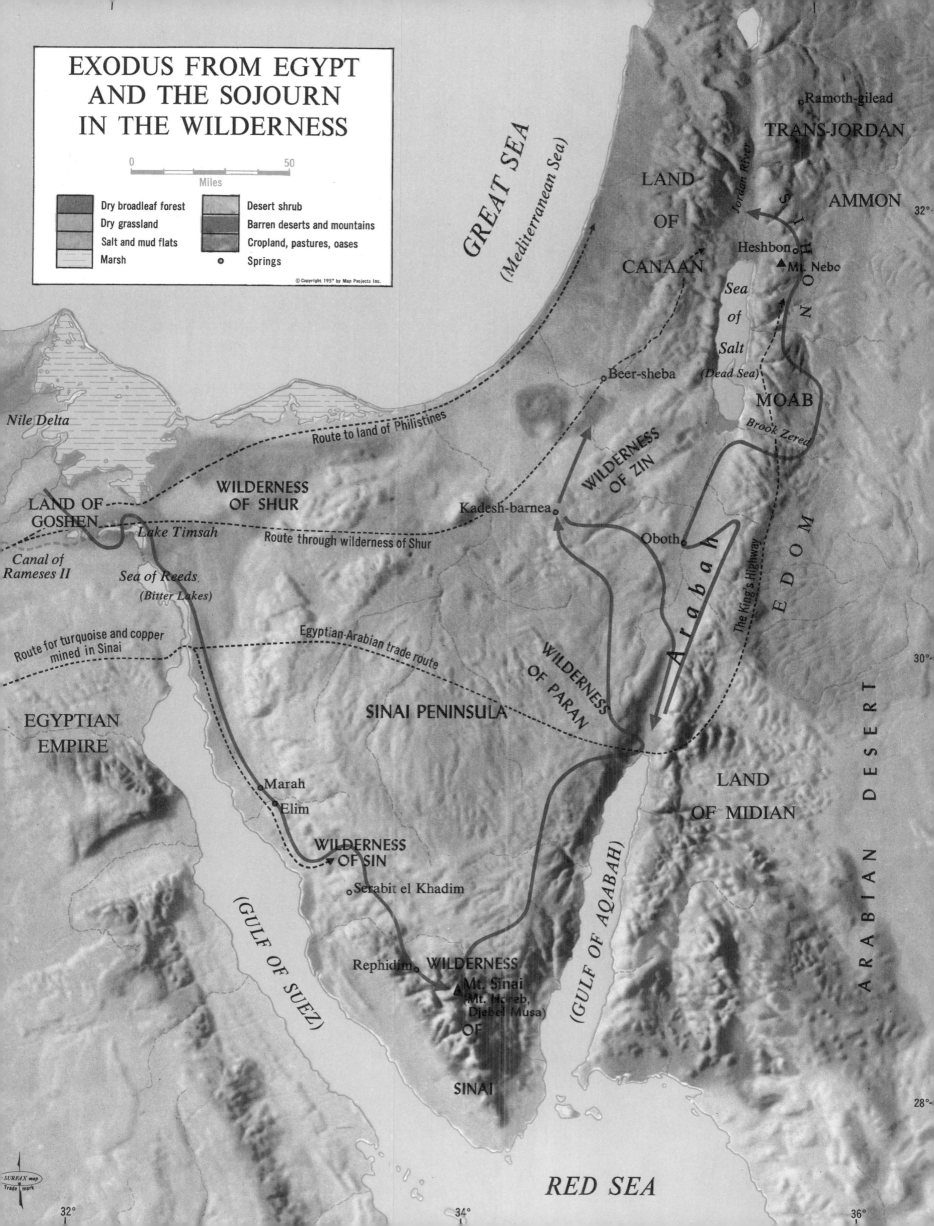

EXODUS FROM EGYPT AND THE SOJOURN IN THE WILDERNESS

0   50
Miles

© Copyright 1957 by Map Projects Inc.

Dry broadleaf forest
Dry grassland
Salt and mud flats
Marsh
Desert shrub
Barren deserts and mountains
Cropland, pastures, oases
○ Springs

GREAT SEA
(Mediterranean Sea)

○ Ramoth-gilead

TRANS-JORDAN

AMMON

LAND OF CANAAN

Heshbon ○

▲ Mt. Nebo

Sea of Salt
(Dead Sea)

MOAB

Brook Zered

Beer-sheba ○

WILDERNESS OF ZIN

Kadesh-barnea ○

Oboth ○

Arabah

The King's Highway

EDOM

Nile Delta

WILDERNESS OF SHUR

LAND OF GOSHEN

Lake Timsah

Route to land of Philistines

Route through wilderness of Shur

Canal of Rameses II

Sea of Reeds
(Bitter Lakes)

Route for turquoise and copper mined in Sinai

Egyptian-Arabian trade route

WILDERNESS OF PARAN

EGYPTIAN EMPIRE

SINAI PENINSULA

LAND OF MIDIAN

ARABIAN DESERT

Marah ○

○ Elim

WILDERNESS OF SIN

○ Serabit el Khadim

(GULF OF SUEZ)

(GULF OF AQABAH)

Rephidim ○   WILDERNESS

▲ Mt. Sinai
(Mt. Horeb, Djebel Musa)

OF

SINAI

RED SEA

SURFAX map
Trade mark

32°   34°   36°

32°
30°
28°

red, on the borderline between Edom and Moab, and then started north again.

At this point the hostile army of Sihon the Amorite, king of Heshbon, came out to meet them. This time the Hebrews fought and won.

Reaching Transjordan (the territory to the east of the Jordan valley), the Israelites were now at the very gates of Canaan. Some of the Hebrews were quite happy to settle down in Transjordan and go no farther.

THE DEATH OF MOSES

Moses was at last nearing the end of his life. As the aged leader stood on the summit of Mount Nebo in Transjordan, where he was to die, he could look down on the northern shore of the Dead Sea and the lush valley of the Jordan. His ancient eyes could survey the whole mountain range of Canaan, from Beer-sheba in the far south to the snowy majesty of Mount Hermon in the far north. He saw the land, but he did not enter it.

With the death of Moses, the forty and more years of wandering in the wilderness were over. The invasion of Canaan was about to begin.

THE HEBREWS IN TRANSJORDAN

Now the Hebrews began to move south again, toward the Gulf of Aqabah. There they intended to turn eastward through the land of Edom on "the King's Highway." However, the Edomites did not grant the Hebrews permission to use this road, and Moses preferred not to risk a battle. Instead, the people marched north along the rocky bottom of the low valley called the Arabah, which joins the Gulf of Aqabah to the Dead Sea.

At the spring of Oboth, not far from the Dead Sea, they tried to cross the land of Moab to the northeast. Permission was refused, and the Hebrews moved eastward along the brook Ze-

The wilderness of Sinai, through which Moses led the Hebrews.

THE INVASION OF CANAAN

ABOUT 1235–1200 B.C.

Joshua and *Judges*, Chapters 1 and 2

Canaanite god

Aᶠᵗᵉʳ ᵗʰᵉ death of Moses —so reports the *Book of Joshua*—the Hebrews encamped at Abel-shittim, on their way down from the high plateau of Transjordan to the low Jordan valley.

THE FALL OF JERICHO AND AI

Across the river, at the foot of the mountains of Canaan, stood the fortress of Jericho. From Abel-shittim, Joshua sent a scouting party to Jericho. When the scouts came back with a favorable report, the Hebrews crossed the Jordan and encamped on the west side, at Gilgal. From there, they stormed the walls of Jericho and took the city. Its fall gave them an entering wedge into the whole of Canaan.

Archaeologists have made several attempts to reconstruct the history of Jericho and to fix the exact date of its destruction. All they have proved is that it was one of the most ancient sites of history. No trace of the Hebrew victory has been found.

Once Jericho was captured, the way was open to the heart of the country. The central mountain range of Canaan was defended by the fortress-city of Ai. Joshua's first attempt to take Ai ended in failure, but he devised a new plan.

Under the cover of night, he sent a detachment of trusted warriors to the mountains west of the city, where they concealed themselves. In the morning, he led the main body of his army openly to the north of Ai, and encamped there in full view. The king of Ai came out of the city with his soldiers to give battle to the Hebrews, who pretended to flee eastward to the Jordan valley. The fortress of Ai was left undefended.

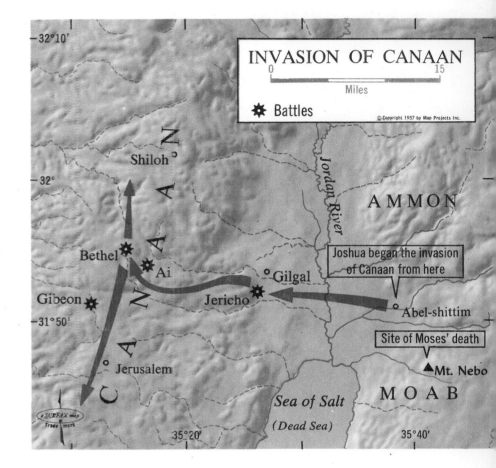

The Hebrews who had waited in ambush to the west of the town moved swiftly forward, stormed the walls, and set fire to the houses. As the smoke rose high in the sky, the king of Ai and his army saw that they had been tricked. Hurrying back, they were caught in the pincers of the Hebrew ambush on one side and the main Hebrew forces on the other.

THE BATTLE OF GIBEON

According to the Biblical account, the inhabitants of Gibeon and several other cities near Ai were so impressed by Israel's victories that they made an offer of peace. Joshua accepted the offer, but he made them slaves—"hewers of wood and drawers of water."

25

Unlike the Gibeonites and their friends, the Amorite king of Jerusalem decided to resist the Hebrew invaders. He made a military alliance with the kings of Hebron, Jarmuth, Lachish, and Eglon. Together, the five kings brought their armies against the city of Gibeon.

The Gibeonites promptly sent to Joshua for help. From Gilgal, deep in the Jordan valley, Joshua made a forced march at night with his warriors. Taken by surprise, the Amorites were thrown into panic and fled. Joshua pursued them down the slopes of Beth-horon. During this famous battle, according to the Bible story, Joshua called upon the sun to stand still at Gibeon and the moon to remain high over the vale of Aijalon, giving enough light for him to take full vengeance on the enemy.

JOSHUA'S SOUTHERN AND NORTHERN CAMPAIGNS

The *Book of Joshua* tells how Israel embarked upon a systematic plan of conquest in the southwest and south of Canaan. One after another, in the hills of the Shephelah toward the seacoast, the fortresses fell: Libnah, Lachish, Eglon. The Hebrews then turned back to the mountain range and moved southward to the cities of Hebron and Debir (Kirjath-sepher). From there, lightning thrusts were made toward the Negeb in the far south, near the oasis of Kadesh-barnea, where the previous generation of Hebrews had stayed many years. The armies also pushed to the far west, toward Gaza near the Mediterranean seacoast.

Archaeological excavations at Lachish (the modern Tell ed-Duweir) prove that the city was completely destroyed in the year 1230 B.C.

Asher
Naphtali
Benjamin
Zebulun
Issachar
Manasseh
Ephraim
Gad
Dan
Judah
Reuben
Simeon

According to the Bible, the land of Canaan was divided among the Twelve Tribes, which bear the names of Jacob's twelve sons.

A profile of the land of Canaan cut from west to east. It was into this land of tall mountains and deep valleys that Joshua marched at the head of the Hebrews.

Scale in feet

5000
4000
3000
2000
1000

Joppa →

Plain

Mediterranean Sea Level

Bethlehem
Judah
Mountain Region

Mt. Nebo
Eastern
Tableland

1000
2000
3000

Jordan Valley at Jericho

Level of Dead Sea
(1300 feet below Mediterranean)

0   10   15   20   25

Scale in miles

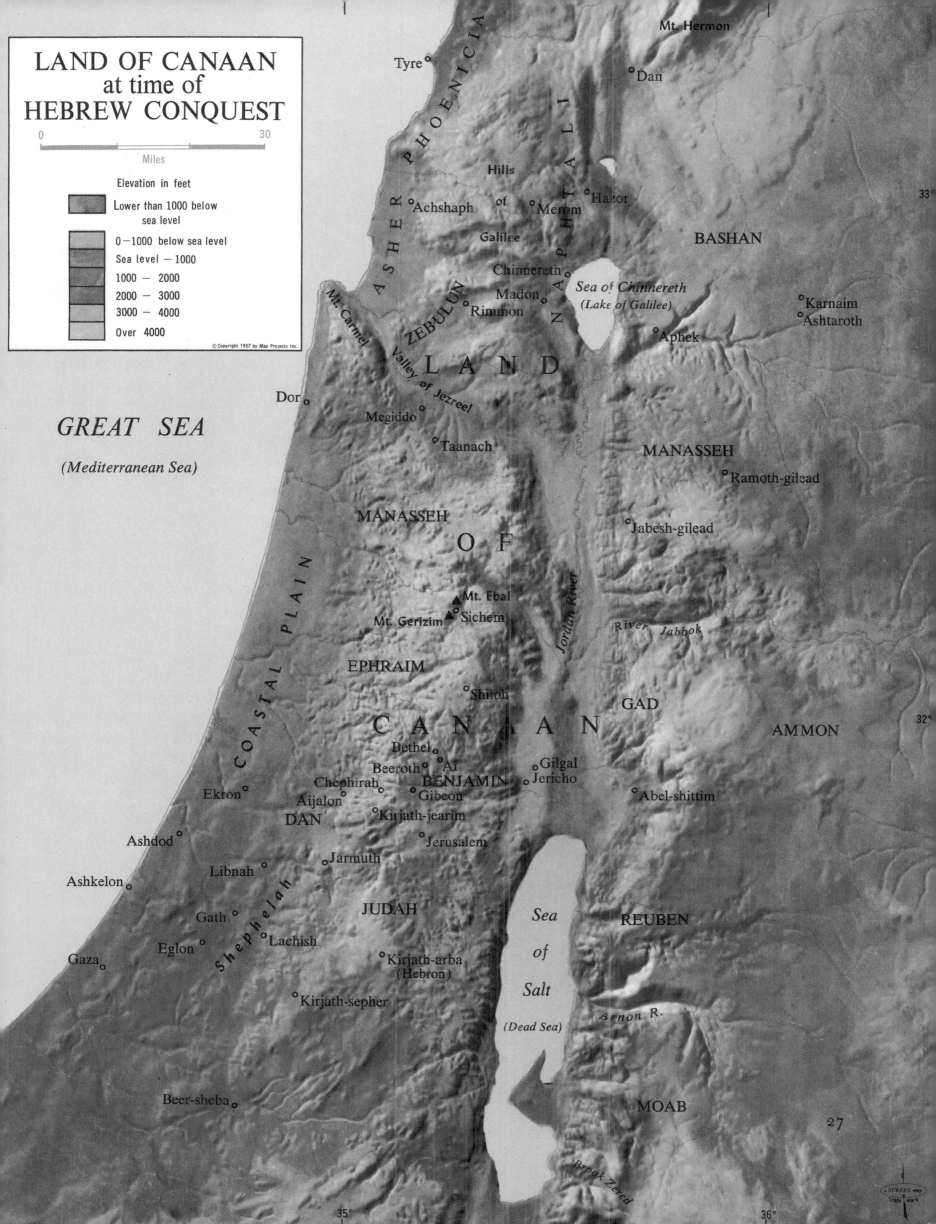

LAND OF CANAAN at time of HEBREW CONQUEST

0 — 30
Miles

Elevation in feet

Lower than 1000 below sea level

0 — 1000 below sea level

Sea level — 1000

1000 — 2000

2000 — 3000

3000 — 4000

Over 4000

© Copyright 1957 by Map Projects Inc.

Mt. Hermon

Tyre

Dan

PHOENICIA

ASHER

Hills of

Achshaph

Merom

Hazor

NAPHTALI

BASHAN

Galilee

Chinnereth

Sea of Chinnereth
(Lake of Galilee)

Karnaim
Ashtaroth

ZEBULUN

Madon

Rimmon

Mt. Carmel

Aphek

L A N D

Dor

Valley of Jezreel

GREAT SEA

(Mediterranean Sea)

Megiddo

Taanach

MANASSEH

Ramoth-gilead

MANASSEH

O F

Jabesh-gilead

COASTAL PLAIN

Jordan River

River Jabbok

Mt. Ebal

Mt. Gerizim

Sichem

EPHRAIM

GAD

Shiloh

C A N A A N

AMMON

Bethel

Ai

Gilgal

Ekron

Beeroth

BENJAMIN

Jericho

Chephirah

Gibeon

Abel-shittim

Aijalon

DAN

Kirjath-jearim

Ashdod

Jerusalem

Jarmuth

Libnah

Ashkelon

Sea

Gath

JUDAH

REUBEN

of

Eglon

Lachish

Shephelah

Gaza

Kirjath-arba
(Hebron)

Salt

Kirjath-sepher

Arnon R.

(Dead Sea)

Beer-sheba

MOAB

27

Brook Zered

33°

32°

35°

36°

A reconstruction from archaeological findings of the fortress of Lachish before its destruction by Joshua. The temple is seen near the center.

Hearing of the Hebrew successes, the Canaanite rulers of the north formed another alliance for defense. The kings of Madon, Shimronmeron, and Achshaph, together with other tribes from the northern hills on both sides of the Lake of Galilee, joined forces near the waters of Merom at the foot of Mount Hermon, near the sources of the Jordan.

As usual, Joshua did not wait for their attack. Boldly marching northward, he gave battle without warning, defeated the enemy forces, and burned the city of Hazor to the ground. From this victory, the Hebrews collected a large booty.

THE CONQUEST FROM THE SOUTH

Although the Hebrews conquered much of Canaan, not all of the country fell into their hands. The *Book of Joshua* is silent about many Canaanite fortresses. Gezer and Jerusalem, in the mountain range, were not occupied until two centuries later. The Canaanites also kept many other strongholds.

Even after Joshua's death—so the *Book of Judges* tells us—the towns of Hebron and Debir,

previously reported as having been taken by Joshua, were still under Canaanite rule. These two cities were conquered from the south by the tribes of Judah and Simeon, which had migrated directly from the Sinai Peninsula with some of their friends, the nomadic clan of the Kenites.

THE MERNEPTAH INSCRIPTION

Along with managing to keep many fortresses in their control, the Canaanites may also have appealed to their overlords, the Egyptians, for help. On the monument of the Pharaoh Merneptah (about 1224–1216 B.C.), in the midst of a description of the Pharaoh's military triumphs over the peoples of the Fertile Crescent, appear these words:

"Israel is desolate: it has no more children! The country is now a widow."

The Pharaoh was mistaken: it was not the end of the people of Israel. Slowly, stubbornly—sometimes with the inevitable cruelty that accompanies warfare—the Israelites established themselves in the land of Canaan.

War chariot

THE TIME OF THE JUDGES

ABOUT 1200–1050 B.C.

Judges, Chapters 3 to 21

THE "JUDGES" of the *Book of Judges* in the Bible were not judges as the word is used today. They were military heroes who rallied the tribes. They were not "kings," because they were not succeeded by their sons.

The period was a troubled one for Israel. Although the Hebrew tribes had gained footholds in the mountains of Canaan, their general situation remained difficult. The Canaanites retained—or regained—the plains and several fortresses which controlled main travel routes.

Thus the plain of Esdraelon (often called Jezreel), between Mount Carmel and Mount Tabor, was in Canaanite hands. In this low, flat region the Hebrew foot soldiers were no match for the Canaanites with their armed horsemen and iron chariots. As a result, the Hebrew tribes of Issachar, Zebulon, and Naphtali, in the Galilee hills, were cut off from the other peoples of the nation, who lived in the central mountain range.

DEBORAH AND THE BATTLE OF ESDRAELON

The prophetess Deborah saw that something had to be done. Although she lived some distance south of Jezreel, between Bethel and Ramah, this remarkable woman managed to assemble a large Hebrew army. She also persuaded Barak, of the Naphtali tribe, to take command. From Mount Tabor, Barak moved against the Canaanite forces under Sisera.

As the battle began, a violent thunderstorm flooded the valley and turned the soil to mud. Sisera's chariots bogged down near the torrent Kishon, at the foot of Mount Carmel. The Canaanites were badly beaten, and Sisera slain. The victory allowed Israel to take the important mountain passes of Taanach and Megiddo.

About this time, a change was taking place in Hebrew life. After living for generations as nomads and shepherds in the desert, Hebrews were now, in this agricultural country, becoming farmers and craftsmen. Also, they were being influenced by the Canaanite religion. Instead of worshiping the one god Yahweh, who could not be represented by a man-made image, farmers were making sacrifices to the "Baalim," or "lords," of the fields. Many Israelites were now forgetting the solemn covenant of Mount Sinai. The *Book of Judges* thus accounts for the misfortunes that befell Israel for nearly two centuries after Joshua.

Besides the Canaanites, the Hebrews also had to fight several nomadic peoples who tried to invade Canaan from the desert, as they themselves had done. The Midianites, for instance, made raids from Transjordan into the central mountain range of Palestine.

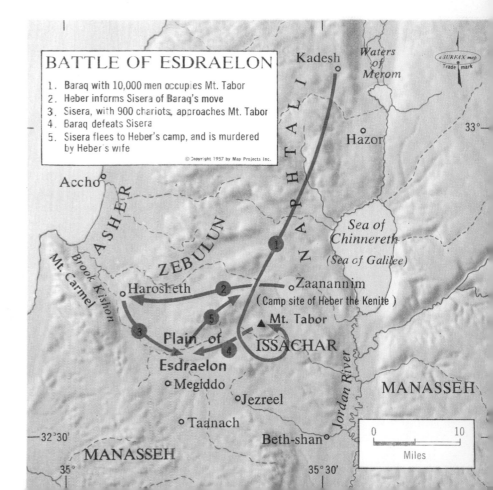

BATTLE OF ESDRAELON

1. Baraq with 10,000 men occupies Mt. Tabor
2. Heber informs Sisera of Baraq's move
3. Sisera, with 900 chariots, approaches Mt. Tabor
4. Baraq defeats Sisera
5. Sisera flees to Heber's camp, and is murdered by Heber's wife

© Copyright 1957 by Map Projects Inc.

Like all nomads, the Hebrews were masters of the art of weaving.

But Gideon, a native of Ophrah, inspired three hundred of his countrymen to attack the Midianites. Following them across the Jordan valley, he and his men surprised the enemy in a strategic night attack. The Hebrews carried lighted torches concealed in pitchers. At a signal from Gideon, they took out the torches and threw away the pitchers. The Midianites thought that a great army had come upon them. They fled in panic and for many years after that left Israel alone.

Two Hebrew cities in Transjordan, Succoth and Penuel, which had been settled by members of Gideon's own tribe, had refused him food and water in his pursuit of the Midianites. On his way home, Gideon punished these cities.

Gideon refused a crown because he thought that Yahweh alone should be king over Israel. After Gideon's death, however, one of his seventy sons, a man named Abimelech, schemed to become king at Shechem. Abimelech soon made himself hated, and was killed by a millstone which a woman dropped on him.

Many years later, in Gilead, there arose a hero named Jephthah. Driven from home by his half brothers, Jephthah had become a highway robber. When the people of Gilead had trouble with the Ammonites, however, they sent for Jephthah and made him their leader. He beat the Ammonites, but a terrible vow forced him to offer up his own daughter in sacrifice.

In the meantime, still other peoples were coming down into Canaan from Asia Minor. Among these were the Philistines, who built strong cities at Ekron, Ashdod, Ashkelon, Gaza, and Gath. They began to push into the Shephelah hills, and forced the tribe of Dan to migrate far north near Mount Hermon.

Samson, a mighty warrior of Mahaneh-dan in the Shephelah, fought the Philistines vigorously for years, until he was betrayed by the Philistine woman Delilah. He was captured, blinded, and taken to Gaza. But there, the Bible tells us, his strength returned, and he pulled down the temple of the Philistine god Dagon, dying with the Philistines in its ruins.

Corrupted by the idol worship of the Canaanites and menaced by new enemies, Israel was entering one of the darkest periods in its history.

The olive press was used for making olive oil. Baskets filled with olives were set upon special rocks. Heavy stones crushed the olives. The oil from them ran through the woven baskets and into holes carved in the rocks. It was then stored in jars. Similar presses were used for making wine.

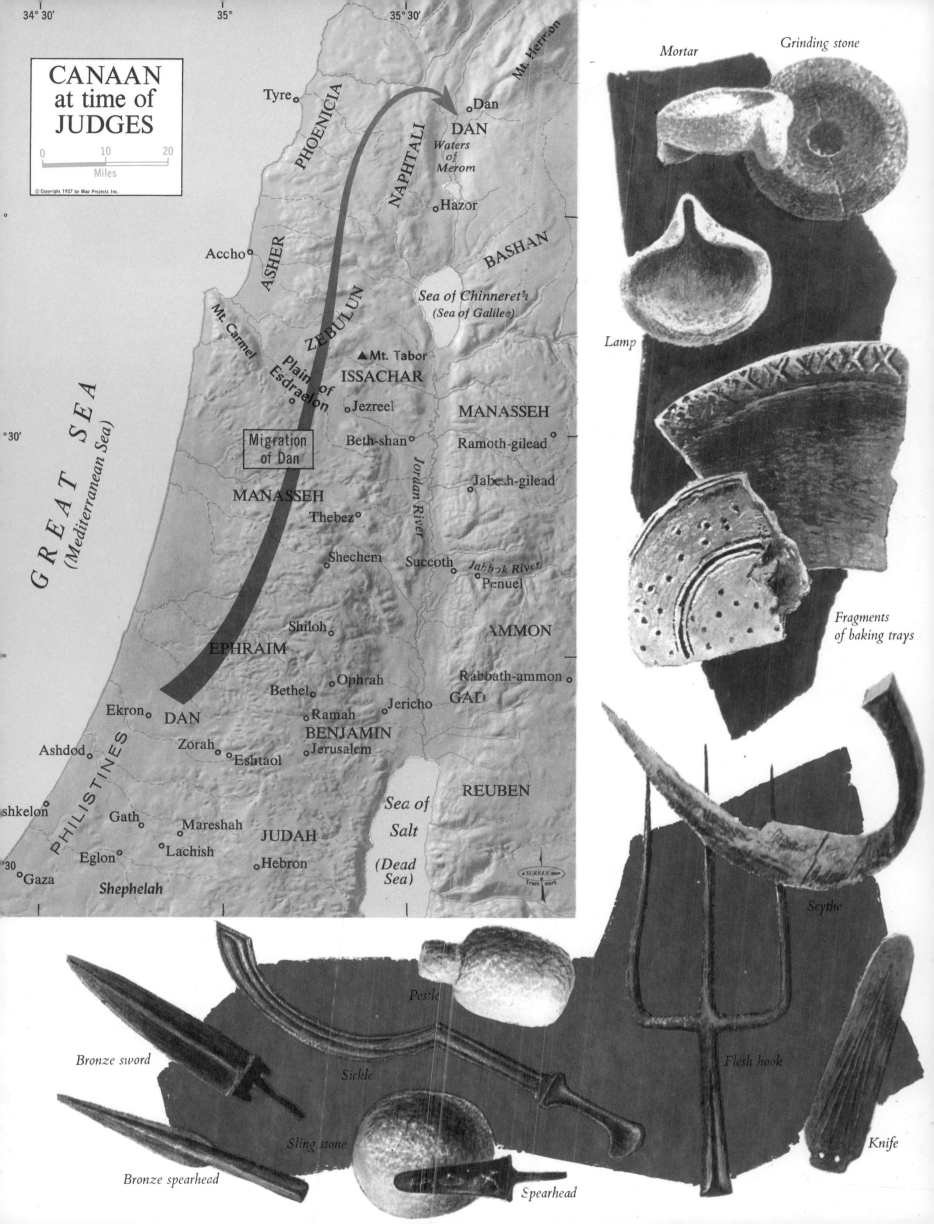

CANAAN at time of JUDGES

© Copyright 1957 by Map Projects Inc.

0   10   20
Miles

GREAT SEA
(Mediterranean Sea)

PHOENICIA

Tyre

Mt. Hermon

Dan

DAN
Waters
of
Merom

NAPHTALI

Hazor

ASHER

Accho

BASHAN

Sea of Chinnereth
(Sea of Galilee)

ZEBULUN

Mt. Carmel

Plain of
Esdraelon

▲ Mt. Tabor

ISSACHAR

Jezreel

MANASSEH

Migration
of Dan

Beth-shan

Ramoth-gilead

MANASSEH

Jabesh-gilead

Jordan River

Thebez

Shechem

Succoth

Jabbok River

Penuel

AMMON

Shiloh

EPHRAIM

Ophrah

Rabbath-ammon

Bethel

GAD

Ekron

DAN

Ramah

Jericho

Zorah

BENJAMIN

Jerusalem

Eshtaol

Ashdod

REUBEN

shkelon

Sea
of
Salt

(Dead
Sea)

Gath

Mareshah

JUDAH

Eglon

Lachish

Gaza

Hebron

Shephelah

a SURFAX more
Trade mark

Mortar

Grinding stone

Lamp

Fragments
of baking trays

Scythe

Bronze sword

Pestle

Sickle

Flesh hook

Sling stone

Knife

Bronze spearhead

Spearhead

Lyre

THE KINGDOM OF SAUL

ABOUT 1050–1002 B.C.

I Samuel, Chapters 1 to 28

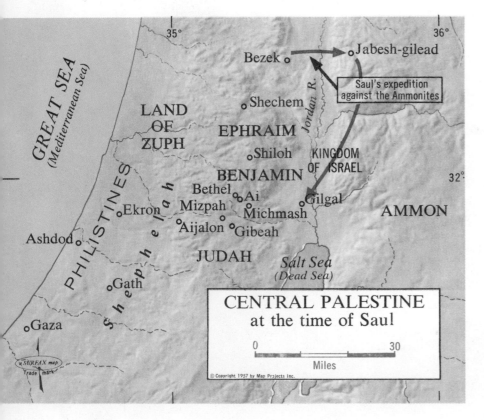
Slinger

DURING THE first half of the eleventh century (1100–1050) B.C., the Philistines conquered the Shephelah hills and often successfully invaded the central mountain range as well. In the country of Ephraim and Benjamin, the conquerors did not allow the Hebrews to sharpen their own plows and scythes for fear that they might also sharpen swords and spears. The most sacred object belonging to the Hebrews, the Ark of the Covenant, was captured in battle by the Philistines, and held for a while by them.

SAMUEL AND SAUL

Even in those dark days, however, one man kept alive the spirit of Israel. He was the prophet Samuel (about 1050–1020 B.C.), of Ramah in

CENTRAL PALESTINE
at the time of Saul

the land of Zuph. Dedicated to a religious life by a pious mother, Samuel was brought up in the temple of Shiloh with the priest Eli. It was during his youth that the Ark of the Covenant, taken from the temple in an effort to win a battle against the Philistines, was captured by the enemy.

Samuel became a "judge" among the Hebrews almost in the modern sense of the word. He administered justice among the tribes of Israel, going every year on a circuit to Bethel, Gilgal, and Mizpah.

The *First Book of Samuel* gives two versions of the great change that came about among the Hebrews during Samuel's time. They wanted to have a king. According to one story, the chiefs of the tribes came to Samuel and asked him to appoint a king who would govern them "like all the nations." Samuel opposed the plan, warning the people how a king could oppress them. He yielded, however, probably because the political situation was desperate. Only a united Israel could throw off the Philistine yoke; and only a king, sanctioned by a man of God, could unite Israel. So Samuel anointed Saul, the son of Kish, from Gibeah. The tribes then gathered together to select Saul publicly at a solemn assembly in Mizpah.

Another story says that Nahash, king of the Ammonites, besieged the Hebrew city of Jabesh-gilead in Transjordan. Its inhabitants sent across the Jordan to the tribe of Benjamin for help. Coming back from the fields behind his oxen, the farmer Saul heard the news. He gathered the warriors of Israel at Bezek, crossed the Jordan valley, and defeated the Ammonites. On the way home, at the sanctuary of Gilgal, he was made king by the grateful people.

THE BATTLE OF MICHMASH

Saul's first task was to clear the Philistines out of the central mountain range. He seems to have been forced into action by his son Jonathan, who defeated a Philistine garrison in Geba. The Philistines sent a punitive force to Michmash, next door to Gibeah, where Saul was encamped. At Michmash there is a high, rocky pass. While Saul, surrounded by six hundred of his warriors, hesitated beneath a pomegranate tree outside of Gibeah, Jonathan daringly climbed the steep slope to Michmash "on hands and feet." He was followed only by his armor-bearer. The two young men overcame the sentinels and spread panic in the enemy camp. Saul's warriors were watching from Gibeah. When they saw what was happening, they fell upon the Philistines and chased them as far as Aijalon.

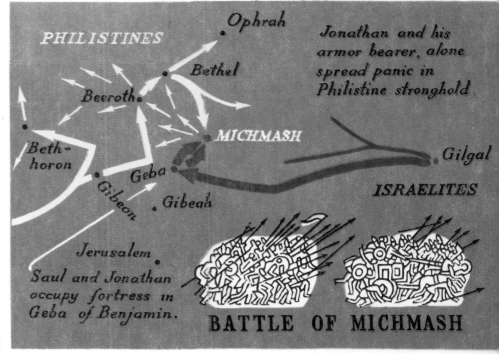

BATTLE OF MICHMASH

THE RISE OF DAVID

For many years, Saul fought against the Philistines. The later part of his life, however, was embittered by the growing popularity of a young shepherd named David. The son of Jesse of Bethlehem, David had defeated a Philistine giant in combat and thus was brought to Saul's court in Gibeah. He was a young man of unusual charm. At court, he became the best friend of Saul's son, Jonathan, and married one of Saul's daughters.

He also became the king's musician, playing on the lyre to soothe Saul, who suffered from spells of mental illness.

It was not long before the mentally sick king turned fiercely on his young rival, and David had to flee for his own life. Escaping by way of Nob, where he was helped by the local priests, he tried to take refuge with the Philistine king of Gath. But the Philistines were suspicious, and David fled again, this time to the cave of Adullam. There he met his parents, whom he took to safety in the land of Moab on the other side of the Dead Sea.

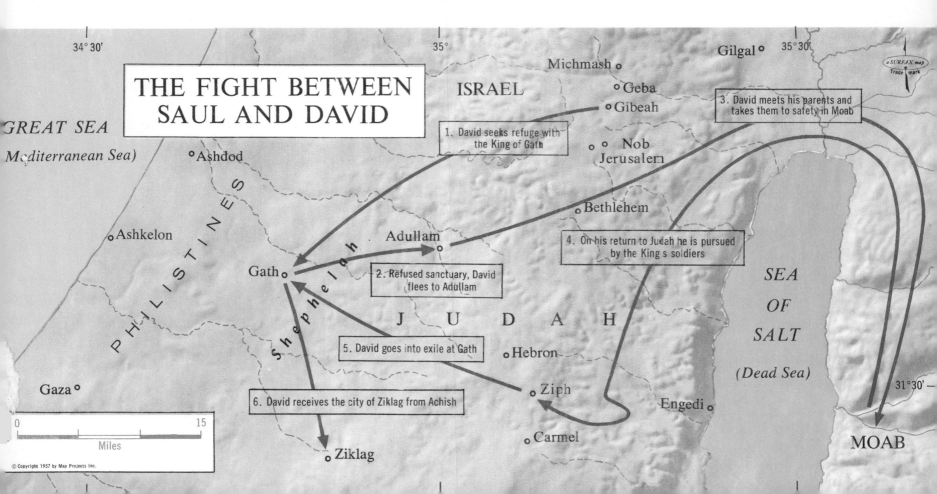

THE FIGHT BETWEEN SAUL AND DAVID

1. David seeks refuge with the King of Gath
2. Refused sanctuary, David flees to Adullam
3. David meets his parents and takes them to safety in Moab
4. On his return to Judah he is pursued by the King's soldiers
5. David goes into exile at Gath
6. David receives the city of Ziklag from Achish

GREAT SEA (Mediterranean Sea)

PHILISTINES

ISRAEL

JUDAH

SEA OF SALT (Dead Sea)

MOAB

0 — 15 Miles

© Copyright 1957 by Map Projects Inc.

The Philistines now got together a new army at Aphek in the plain of Sharon, and marched through the plain of Jezreel toward Shunem to fight Saul. Some of the Philistines still distrusted David, and he was not forced to fight on their side in the battle.

Saul went north to meet the Philistines, and encamped with his army on Mount Gilboa. He was an old man now, without David's help and without the advice of the prophet Samuel, who had died some years before.

In his desperation, Saul broke his own law. Loyal to Yahweh, he had forbidden witchcraft throughout Israel, as Canaanite superstition. But now he disguised himself and visited a witch at En-dor, to consult the ghost of Samuel. All he learned was that God had deserted him.

The next day, the battle was fought—and lost. Three of the king's sons, among them Jonathan, were slain. Saul himself, recognized from afar by the Philistine archers, was wounded by an arrow. To avoid capture and death at the hands of his enemies, he fell on his own sword. And so ended the life of the first king of Israel, surely one of the most tragic figures of the Old Testament.

Nebi Samuwil, where Moslems today venerate "the grave of Samuel."

Returning to the land of his own tribe of Judah, David was constantly pursued by the king's soldiers. From the wilderness of Ziph he had to move further south to the desert of Maon, and down to the Arabah, beyond the borders of Saul's kingdom.

David next went to Engedi, in the desert of Judah just above the Dead Sea, and then back to Ziph. But the Ziphites tried to betray him, and he finally decided to go into exile at Gath in Philistia. By this time, David was the leader of a band of about six hundred warriors. Achish, the king of Gath, mindful of future troubles, was glad to give such a promising ally the city of Ziklag for his own.

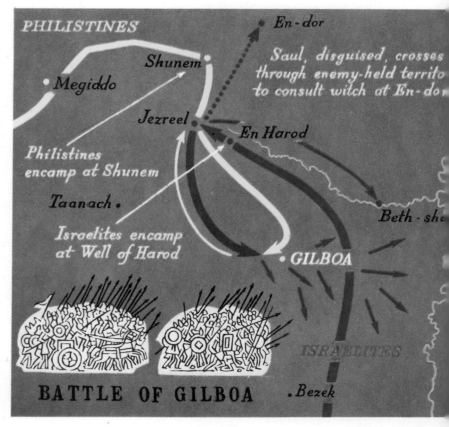

PHILISTINES

En-dor

Saul, disguised, crosses through enemy-held territo to consult witch at En-dor

Shunem

Megiddo

Jezreel

En Harod

Philistines encamp at Shunem

Taanach.

Beth-sh

Israelites encamp at Well of Harod

GILBOA

ISRAELITES

BATTLE OF GILBOA

.Bezek

THE KINGDOM OF DAVID

1002—962 B.C.

II Samuel, Chapters 1 to 24

Ark of the Lord

O<small>N LEARNING</small> that Saul and Jonathan had been killed in the battle of Gilboa, David lamented for them in a dirge which is one of the most beautiful in all literature. It begins:

> *"Thy glory, O Israel, is slain upon thy*
> *high places!*
> *How are the mighty fallen!"*

David immediately left Ziklag with his whole following, and went to Hebron in the land of Judah. There he was anointed king of Judah, the southern part of Palestine.

To drive the Philistines out of the country, the new king had to unite the tribes of the south, the north, and Transjordan. Between the southern and northern tribes, however, a serious rift had already appeared. And now Abner, the commander of Saul's army, took Saul's fourth son, Ishbaal (in the Bible called Ishbosheth), to Mahanaim, and had him declared king of Israel. The result was two years of bloody civil war (1002–1000 B.C.).

At a battle in Gibeon, Abner slew a nephew of David, named Asahel, who was a brother of David's general, Joab. When Abner tried to abandon the weak King Ishbaal and to go over to King David instead, Joab slew Abner by treachery, to avenge the slaying of Asahel.

David publicly mourned for Abner's death and convinced the people that he had no part in it. As a result, northern Israel decided to support David, and he was made king over the whole nation. The force and charm of his personality healed, for a generation, the breach between the south and the north.

THE CAPTURE OF JERUSALEM

With rare political sense, David saw that Hebron was too much a part of the "south" to be an acceptable capital to all Israel. He needed a city that was neither "south" nor "north." For this purpose the old stronghold of Jerusalem, still held by the Canaanites, was ideal. Halfway between Saul's capital of Gibeah and David's own birthplace at Bethlehem, it was a natural fortress. Neither Joshua nor any other Hebrew leader had been able to conquer it.

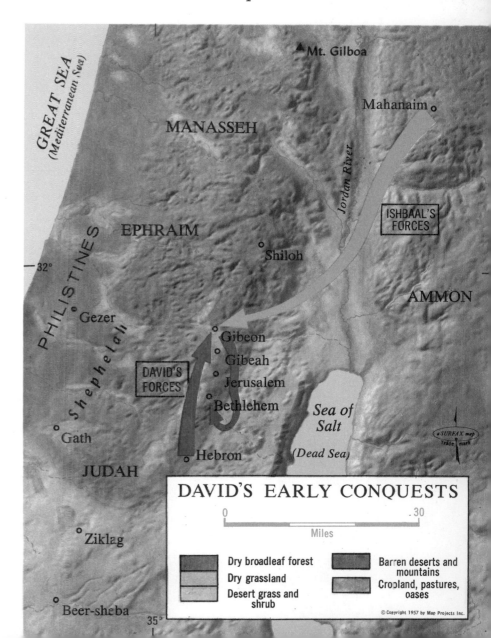

DAVID'S EARLY CONQUESTS

0   .30

Miles

Dry broadleaf forest

Dry grassland

Desert grass and shrub

Barren deserts and mountains

Cropland, pastures, oases

© Copyright 1957 by Map Projects Inc.

Horizontal plan of the tunnel

Spring of Gihon

Cross section

David took it by making his attack through a tunnel used to bring water into the city.

The new ruler soon put aside a holy place for worshiping the God of Israel. On the northern plateau he bought a threshing-floor—a large rock platform—where he built an altar for the offering of sacrifices to the Lord. In solemn procession, he brought the ancient Ark of the Sinai desert to Jerusalem. The Ark became a symbol of national unity and of loyalty to the Lord.

David wanted to build a temple for the Ark, but the prophet Nathan kept him from doing it. Nathan represented the old religious ideas of

When David's army laid siege to Jerusalem, all the Canaanite warriors were posted on the walls. To the blind and the lame went the task of guarding the tunnel through which water could be brought in from the spring of Gihon outside the walls. But David sent a raiding party through the tunnel, and thus Jerusalem was taken.

the nomadic Hebrews, for whom "God does not sit, but walks." However, David built a palace for himself, his wives, and his many children; and he strengthened the defenses of the citadel, which became known as "the city of David."

DAVID AND THE PHILISTINES

The Philistines quickly saw that David was a threat to them. They sent an army which encamped a few miles from Jerusalem in the valley of Rephaim, among the "mulberry trees."

David did not attack the Philistine camp by way of the natural opening of the valley. Instead, he made a long detour by Gibeah and the high point of Gibeon. When the wind shifted so that David's advance patrols could hear the noise of the Philistine camp among the trees, he swooped down upon the enemy and chased them as far as Gezer in the Shephelah.

The struggle with the Philistines went on for several years. David's bodyguard of warriors, "the thirty and the three," often fought the most gigantic of the Philistines in single combat, as David himself had once fought Goliath. Little

On this rock David offered sacrifices. Later Solomon built the temple on it. Today it is enclosed by a mosque called the Dome of the Rock.

36

by little, the Philistines were driven back. Israel took over Gath and Ziklag, where David had lived in exile.

David's great gifts of leadership and personal charm even won over some of his defeated enemies. In his army were not only Hebrews, but also Philistines, especially the Cherethites (possibly from the island of Crete), the Pelethites, and the Gittites (from Gath).

DAVID'S WARS OF CONQUEST

To get money for his building projects in Jerusalem and for his professional army, David embarked upon a program of conquest. With loot, tribute, and the slave labor of war prisoners, he balanced the government budget. He defeated the Moabites, killing some and enslaving the rest. He defeated the Edomites in the Valley of Salt not far from Beer-sheba, and slew the entire royal family of Edom except for Hadad, a prince who fled to Egypt. Edom became a part of the province of Judah.

In Transjordan, David fought the Ammonites; but the Ammonites proved harder to conquer. They hired Syrian soldiers, horsemen, and iron chariots from Damascus. When David finally did overcome the Ammonites and Syrians, the operation was profitable. The victory gave him manpower, arms of bronze, and shields of gold. He even set up and maintained garrisons in Damascus itself.

David's wars of conquest had four important results. They strengthened Israel against her greedy neighbors. They filled the royal treasury so that David did not have to tax his own people. They kept the northern tribes from resenting a "southern" ruler. And they gave the king prestige with foreign nations.

David maintained diplomatic relations with the Syrians of Geshur, the Phoenicians of Tyre, and even the northern Syrians of Hamath on the Orontes. He ruled directly, or controlled indirectly, the whole land-bridge or Fertile Crescent, from the Euphrates to the Isthmus of Suez. To be sure, he could do so only because, for the first time in history, Mesopotamia and Egypt were both too weak to interfere.

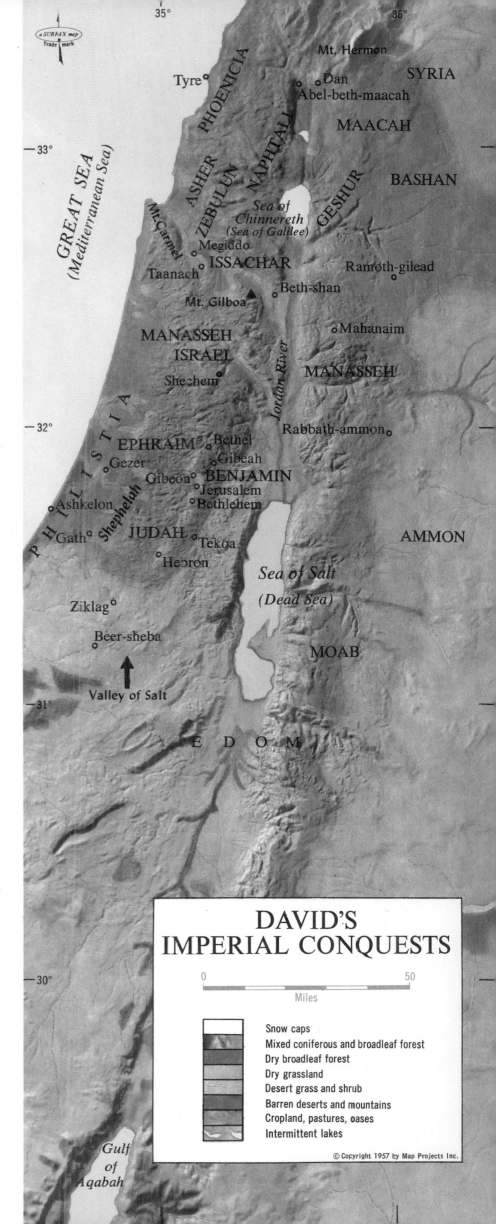

DAVID'S IMPERIAL CONQUESTS

0   50
Miles

☐ Snow caps
◼ Mixed coniferous and broadleaf forest
◼ Dry broadleaf forest
◼ Dry grassland
◼ Desert grass and shrub
◼ Barren deserts and mountains
◼ Cropland, pastures, oases
◼ Intermittent lakes

© Copyright 1957 by Map Projects Inc.

A modern view of Jerusalem from outside its walls. Many cacti grow in the region.

THE REVOLT OF ABSALOM

However, David was having trouble within his own family. He himself set an example of treacherous dealing when he had a faithful captain, Uriah the Hittite, betrayed in battle and killed so that he could steal Uriah's wife, the astonishingly beautiful Bathsheba. A few years later, Amnon, David's eldest son and heir to the throne, fell in love with his half sister Tamar. Absalom, Tamar's brother, killed Amnon, and had to flee into exile among the Syrians of Geshur. After three years, David pardoned him and Absalom returned—to plot against his father.

Gathering a large number of young men around him, particularly from the northern tribes of Benjamin and Ephraim, Absalom had himself declared king at Hebron. Then he and his army of young toughs marched on Jerusalem.

David retreated in haste to Mahanaim. But David's general, Joab, rallied the army and defeated Absalom's forces in the forest of Ephraim. Absalom, fleeing on muleback, was caught by the hair in the branches of a large oak and killed by Joab's men. David returned to Jerusalem mourning for his son—just as he had mourned, years before, at the death of Saul.

DAVID THE MAN AND KING

David was a baffling and many-sided person. Brave and loyal to friends and enemies alike, he was capable of outrageous cruelty and even—as with Uriah—of treachery. He was faithful to the religion of his fathers, humble before the prophet of the Lord, and sometimes carried away by his feelings, as when he danced before the Ark. He was a great poet and musician, a man of war, a statesman, and a romantic hero.

As king, he completed the conquest of Canaan which Joshua had begun more than two centuries before. He restored the unity of the tribes, at least for a time. The Promised Land, dream of the ancient nomads, had at last become a reality.

But one problem had not been solved—who would rule after David's death?

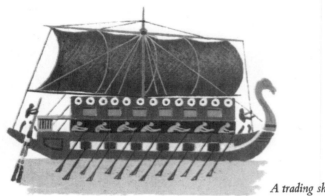

A trading ship

SOLOMON'S EMPIRE

962–922 B.C.

I Kings, Chapters 1 to 11

THE LAST YEARS of David's reign were made sad by drought, famine, and plague. At last the old king lay dying. The question of the next king had to be decided at once.

The princes Amnon and Absalom were dead. Next in line was the handsome Adonijah, who was supported by Joab, commander-in-chief of the army, and Abiathar the priest. Confidently, Adonijah's friends declared him king at the sacred spring, En-rogel, in the Kidron valley just south of Jerusalem.

Queen Bathsheba, however, had other plans. From the dying King David she obtained the promise that her own son Solomon would be the next ruler. Attended by the priest Zadok, the chief of the royal guard Benaiah, and the prophet Nathan, Solomon rode King David's royal mule to the spring of Gihon, just outside the city wall. There, Zadok and Nathan anointed him king of Israel.

After David's death, Solomon wasted no time in getting rid of his enemies. His brother and rival, Adonijah, and the old general Joab were put to death. The priest Abiathar was exiled. The prophet Samuel's fear, that monarchy would bring with it the Oriental pattern of palace intrigue and murder, was unfortunately becoming true.

Ruthless as a politician, Solomon was gifted as an administrator. He divided the kingdom into twelve districts which cut across the ancient tribal boundaries and weakened tribal government. He also imposed a system of forced labor upon his people. At one time the northerners revolted under the leadership of Jeroboam. But the rebellion was crushed, and Jeroboam had to flee to Egypt.

The old Canaanite fortresses of Dor, Megiddo, Taanach, and Beth-shean, controlling the strategic passes around the plain of Jezreel, were woven into Solomon's line of defenses. The stronghold of Gezer, in the Shephelah, came to him as a dowry from Egypt when he married one of the Pharaoh's daughters.

SOLOMON'S INTERNATIONAL ROLE

David won great power for Israel; Solomon used it. To be sure, he suffered setbacks. Hadad the Edomite prince, who had escaped to Egypt when David conquered Edom, came home and regained from Solomon his nation's independence. Likewise, the Syrians of Damascus were hostile all through Solomon's reign.

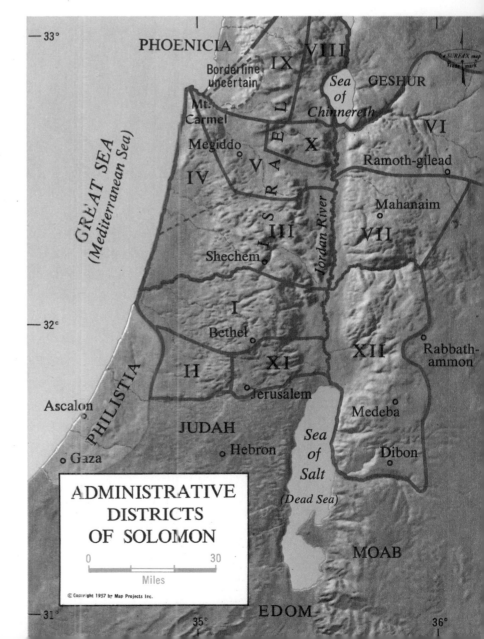

ADMINISTRATIVE DISTRICTS OF SOLOMON

0   30
Miles

© Copyright 1957 by Map Projects Inc.

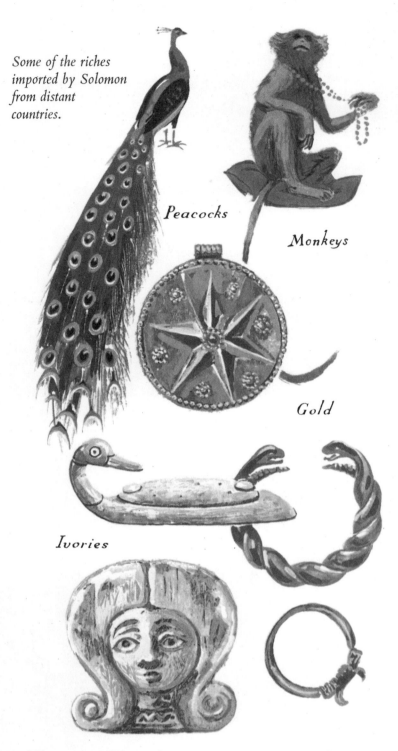

Some of the riches imported by Solomon from distant countries.

Peacocks

Monkeys

Gold

Ivories

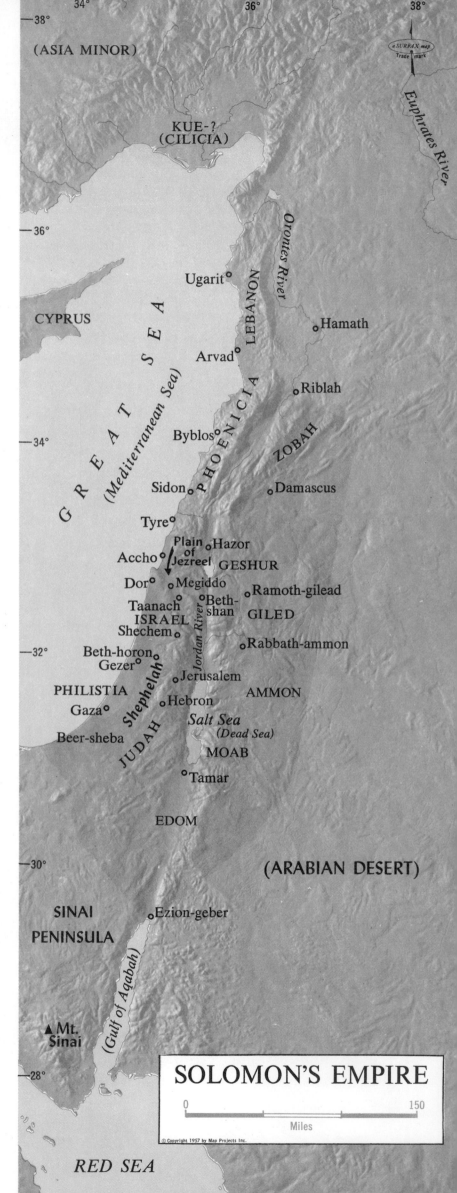

SOLOMON'S EMPIRE

0   150

Miles

© Copyright 1957 by Map Projects Inc.

The new King, better at commerce than at war, traded widely. From Ezion-geber, on the Gulf of Aqabah, his ocean-going ships sailed down the Red Sea to the mysterious "land of Ophir"—perhaps the coast of Zanzibar in Africa, of Malabar in India, or Yemen in southern Arabia. They brought back red sandalwood (almug), precious stones, gold, silver, ivory, spices, monkeys, and peacocks. But Solomon was a metals magnate, too. At Ezion-geber archaeologists have found large smelting furnaces for copper and iron. Solomon's agents also imported horses from Kue (Cilicia), near the Taurus Mountains in Asia Minor, as well as chariots from Egypt.

40

Watering trough

The fortress of Megiddo was a chariot city. Solomon's stables were rebuilt and enlarged by later kings of Israel.

Solomon's foreign connections are shown by the array of foreign princesses he married. One of his most important alliances was with Hiram, the Phoenician king of Tyre. Solomon obtained from Hiram the cypress and cedar wood from Lebanon for the vast building projects which marked his reign.

SOLOMON AS A BUILDER

To store imported and exported goods in transit, Solomon needed large, safe warehouses. He built them in the fortresses which commanded the caravan routes—Hazor and Megiddo on the route between Egypt and Phoenicia; Beth-horon and Gezer on the route between Egypt and Jerusalem; Baalath and Tamar, on the route to the south. At Megiddo were stables for horses.

In Jerusalem, Solomon filled the narrow gap (the Millo) which separated the City of David (Ophel) from the higher plateau to the north; and he built walls to defend the whole area. On the old threshing-floor acquired by David, he erected magnificent palaces for himself, his Egyptian princess, and his other wives. There were also imposing government buildings, such as the House of the Forest of Lebanon (perhaps for the royal guard) and the Hall of Pillars. But Solomon's most ambitious undertaking was the temple of Jerusalem.

SOLOMON'S TEMPLE

The prophet Nathan had opposed David's plan for a temple; now, either he changed his mind or Solomon overruled him. Architects and metal workers were imported from Phoenicia, and the work began.

From copper and iron mined near the Gulf of Aqabah, craftsmen forged many beautiful objects.

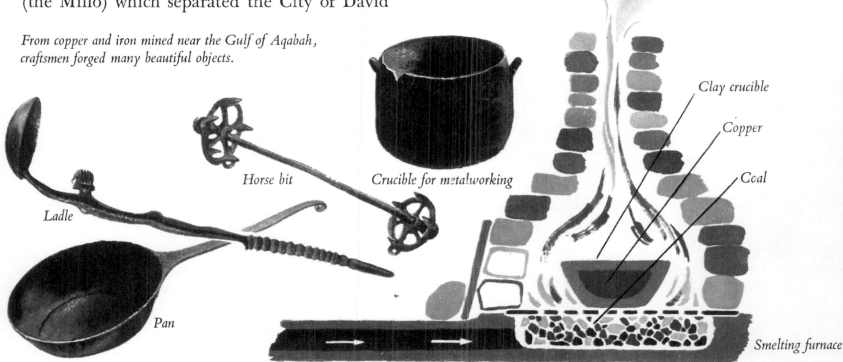

Ladle

Horse bit

Crucible for metalworking

Pan

Clay crucible

Copper

Coal

Smelting furnace

Laver, used to carry water to the great Sea of Bronze.

Inner Sanctuary

Side Chambers

Holy Place

Porch

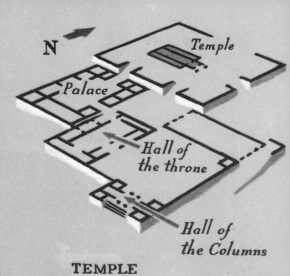

N

Temple

Palace

Hall of the throne

Hall of the Columns

TEMPLE AREA

Copper capital that was placed on columns in front of the temple.

Drawing adapted from a model by Professor Paul L. Garber, Agnes Scott College, Decatur, Ga.

The Sea of Bronze was placed so that the four groups of bulls faced the four points of the compass.

Altar

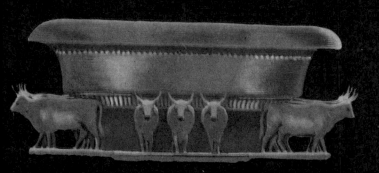

42

Sea of Bronze

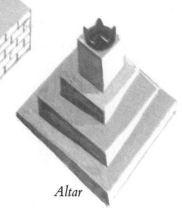

Solomon's Temple, which, it has been said, was "the joy of the whole earth," was built of pure white limestone. The interior was wainscoted with choice cedar from Lebanon's mountain forests.

The temple stood on the north side of the city proper, facing to the east a large courtyard which contained the altar for sacrifices. There stood also the "Sea of Bronze," a huge basin which held ten thousand gallons of water for cleaning the courtyard after the sacrifices.

The temple itself was fairly small. It was only about one hundred feet long, thirty feet wide, and forty-five feet high. To the east was a shallow entrance porch which opened on the courtyard; it led to the main room, or Holy Place. This room was dimly lighted by small latticed windows. It contained an altar for incense, a table for holy bread, and twelve seven-branched candlesticks. The walls, floor, and ceiling were made of precious woods.

From the Holy Place, a flight of stairs led to the third room, the Inner Sanctuary. In this room, shaped like a cube, stood the Ark of the Lord, guarded by two carved cherubim with outspread wings. The room was in utter darkness; a thick curtain at the entrance kept out all light.

Because it had been built by Phoenicians, the temple looked almost exactly like a Phoenician shrine to the sun god. At the ceremony of dedication, Solomon was careful to say, "The Lord has set the sun in the heavens, but has said that he would dwell in thick darkness." That is, Solomon himself tried to keep the temple pure from pagan practices. But with the temple, as with the kingship, the Israelites were becoming more and more like their Canaanite neighbors.

THE WISDOM OF SOLOMON

Solomon's international trade and diplomacy brought to Jerusalem many foreign visitors and sent many Israelites abroad. One of these visitors was the Queen of Sheba.

Solomon became known as one of the wisest of men. Like many other kings of the Near East, he encouraged the men of his court to speak of the meaning of life, of man, and of the world. These thoughts were often phrased in short and witty proverbs. Tradition says that Solomon himself wrote thousands of proverbs.

Wise as he may have been, Solomon did not understand the moral and social ideas behind

Only a few of the cedars of Lebanon remain. Formerly, cedarwood from Lebanon was used for building throughout the ancient world.

the ancient Hebrew faith. The covenant on Mount Sinai was made with all the people, not just with a privileged class. But Solomon's love of power and display did more than bankrupt his country. It also led to a deep change within Israelite society, away from the early democracy and toward tyranny and injustice.

The largest of the so-called Solomon's Pools. These reservoirs continued to supply Jerusalem with water until modern times.

Shishak's victory in Palestine

THE
TWO KINGDOMS

922–850 B.C.

I Kings 12, to II Kings 7

UP TO THE time of Solomon's death in 922 B.C., the whole of Palestine had been known as "Israel." But in 922, the uneasy truce between north and south ended, and the country split permanently apart. The north took over the name of Israel, while the south kept the old name of Judah. Each part, of course, thought of itself as the "true" Hebrew nation.

The reasons for the split were many. The north and the south were different in soil, climate, and geographic location. They were different in culture and history as well. Without a strong, determined ruler, these differences could not be bridged.

Israel, the north, received enough rainfall to grow grain, grapes, and olives. Rich pastures supported good breeds of cattle. But very little could grow in Judah, the dry south. Judah needed to import more than it could export.

Israel lay in the midst of the Fertile Crescent, at the crossroads of the ancient world. Its ties were with Phoenicia, both in trade and in religion. From the Canaanites, the cousins of the Phoenicians, the Israelite farmers had learned to worship the forces of nature and of fertility.

In Judah, on the other hand, there were more shepherds than farmers. People could more easily be faithful to the religion of the old nomadic days. Also, Judah was off the beaten track. It was harder for the people of Judah to learn of pagan customs and ideas.

Finally, the northerners had their own holy shrines—Shechem and Shiloh—and their own old capitals of Gibeah and Mahanaim. They remembered that the "southerner" Solomon had forced many of them into slave labor.

THE REVOLT OF ISRAEL, 922-921 B.C.

Rehoboam, the son of Solomon, became king in Jerusalem; but he had to journey to Shechem, the ancient holy place of the north, to be confirmed by the elders of Israel. At Shechem, the people demanded that he relax the cruel forced labor laws of his father. Rehoboam refused.

Instantly, rebellion flared. Adoram, the king's minister, was stoned to death; Rehoboam himself barely escaped. Jeroboam, the northern rebel who had fled to Egypt under Solomon, was now back in Israel. With the help of Ahijah of Shiloh, a prophet of Yahweh, he became Israel's king.

JUDAH FROM REHOBOAM TO JEHOSHAPHAT

Rehoboam was thus king of Judah only. He spent his entire reign, from 922 to 915 B.C., trying unsuccessfully to regain Israel. The civil war between north and south gave the Pharaoh Shishak a chance to send a military expedition from Egypt up through Palestine and Syria. In 917 Shishak overcame Jerusalem and carried off the treasures of Solomon.

Rehoboam's son Abijam (915–913 B.C.) and grandson Asa (913–873 B.C.) continued the war with Israel. But Jehoshaphat (873–849 B.C.) made peace with the north and turned his attention elsewhere. He reconquered Edom and built a new fleet of ocean-going ships at Ezion-geber. His idea was to regain the wealth of Solomon, but a storm wrecked the fleet before it sailed.

Damascus

Mt. Lebanon

Zarephath

Mt. Hermon

A
R
A
M

SYRIAN INVASIONS

Dan

Tyre

PHOENICIA

33°

Accho

Mts. of Galilee

Sea of Chinnereth
(Sea of Galilee)

Aphek

Brook Kishon

Mt. Carmel

Ramoth-gilead

Dor

Megiddo

Jezreel

I
S
R
A
E
L

Taanach

Beth-shan

Plain of Sharon

Tishbe
Mahanaim

Samaria

Tirzah

Jordan River

Shechem

GREAT SEA
(Mediterranean Sea)

AMMON

Joppa

32°

Shiloh

Bethel

Rabbath-ammon

Gezer

Gibeah

Heshbon

PHILISTIA

Jerusalem

Bethlehem

Sea
of
Salt

JUDAH

(Dead
Sea)

Gaza

Hebron

EGYPTIAN INVASION
UNDER SHISHAK

KINGDOMS OF
ISRAEL AND JUDAH

Beer-sheba

0   30

Miles

Kingdom of Israel
Kingdom of Judah

Kir-hareseth

M
O
A
B

© Copyright 1957 by Map Projects Inc.

35°

36°

31°

EDOM

Egyptian god Bes and gaming board in ivory, from Megiddo.

ISRAEL FROM JEROBOAM TO AHAB

While the kings of Judah were succeeding one another from father to son, the kings of Israel were systematically killing one another.

Jeroboam (922–901 B.C.) needed a capital for his new kingdom. First he fortified Shechem; then he moved to Penuel in Transjordan. He also built temples at Bethel and Dan to show his religious, as well as political, independence.

Jeroboam's son Nadab succeeded him, but in about a year Nadab was murdered by one of his captains, Baasha. Baasha reigned until 877 B.C. and moved the capital of Israel to Tirzah. Baasha's son Elah was also murdered by one of his officers, who reigned seven days before he was overthrown by Omri, a rival captain.

Modern excavations of Samaria's walls and gate show that Omri employed skillful architects. Cisterns provided the city with water.

Omri (877–869 B.C.) was a competent king. First he recaptured almost every fortress in Israel. Then he conquered Moab, set up friendly relations with the Phoenicians, and allied himself with Ethbaal, king of Tyre. He strengthened the alliance by arranging the marriage of his son Ahab to the Tyrian princess Jezebel.

Omri moved the capital of Israel from Tirzah to a new site, Samaria. The new city was well located, on a hill rising above a green valley in the central mountain range.

Ahab (896–850 B.C.) had to fight the Syrians of Damascus, who besieged Samaria under Benhadad II in 855 B.C. They did not take the city, however, and the next year Ahab defeated Benhadad's army at Aphek. He reconquered a number of border towns and secured trading rights in Damascus for his people.

Ahab built for his Phoenician queen a temple dedicated to the Baal of Tyre, and supported pagan priests and prophets at public expense.

THE PROPHET ELIJAH

Early in Ahab's reign, however, the prophet Elijah from Tishbe boldly opposed the worship of Baal. He called the people to Mount Carmel to choose between Yahweh and Baal. He persuaded them to slay the prophets of Baal beside the brook Kishon, where Sisera's chariots had once bogged down. But the queen herself remained a pagan.

Remembering Moses, Elijah made a journey to Mount Sinai (Horeb), in the far south. There, he learned a lesson that became historically important in both Judaism and in Christianity. He learned that God no longer spoke in the earthquake, the lightning, and the whirlwind. God did not make himself known through signs, but through the human voices of his prophets.

When Queen Jezebel had Naboth, a small farmer from Jezreel, put to death because King Ahab wanted Naboth's vineyard for a garden, Elijah reappeared. Angrily he spoke out against the injustice, telling the king that the dogs would lick up his blood and the blood of Jezebel.

Elijah was the first of the great prophets to oppose not only idolatry but social injustice.

THE ASSYRIAN EMPIRE AND THE END OF ISRAEL

850–722 B.C.

*II Kings 8-21, Amos 1-9, Hosea 1-14,
Isaiah 1-39, Micah 1-7*

Sargon and officer before a god

ABOUT THE time of Ahab, a new and terrifying power, Assyria, was rising in the ancient world. The Assyrians had lived for many years in northern Mesopotamia, and had inherited the culture and religion of Babylon. They were a cruel and ferocious people. Their enemies they burned alive or impaled; they built pyramids of human skulls and decorated their palace walls with human skin.

To fight this new enemy, Ahab of Israel and the Syrian Ben-hadad of Damascus joined with other kings in a great league. In 853 B.C., the league waged a battle at Qarqar on the Orontes River. This stopped the Assyrian advances for more than a hundred years.

After the battle, Ahab and Ben-hadad again became enemies, and Elijah's prophecy came true. Ahab was killed by the Syrians at Ramoth-gilead in 850 B.C. Joram, the son who finally succeeded Ahab, had to fight off a Syrian siege of Samaria. Wounded in another battle with the Syrians at Ramoth-gilead, Joram was killed by his own general Jehu, who then became king of Israel and reigned until 815 B.C.

THE REVOLUTION OF JEHU, 842 B.C.

Jehu represented a revolution in Israel—a revolution against Baal idolatry. Supported by the prophet Elisha and the Rechabites, a religious sect from southern Judah, Jehu first got

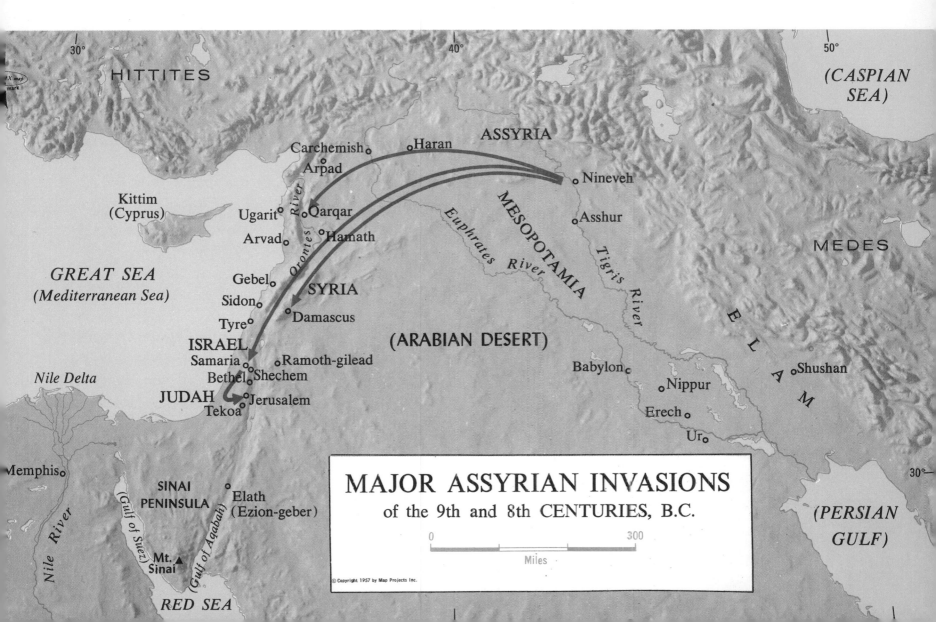

MAJOR ASSYRIAN INVASIONS
of the 9th and 8th CENTURIES, B.C.

0   300

Miles

© Copyright 1957 by Map Projects Inc.

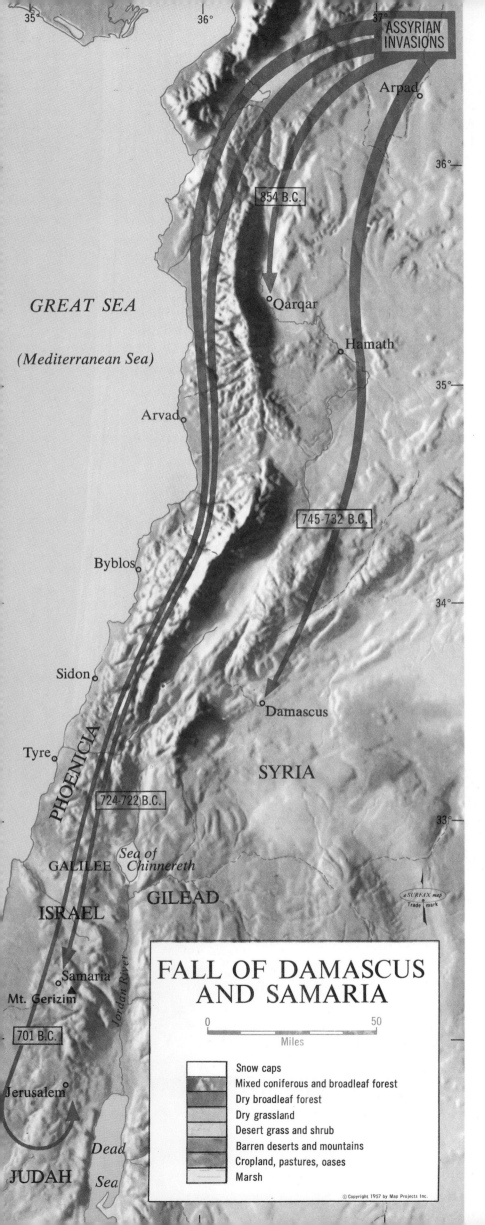

ASSYRIAN
INVASIONS

Arpad

854 B.C.

Qarqar

Hamath

GREAT SEA

(Mediterranean Sea)

Arvad

745-732 B.C.

Byblos

Sidon

Damascus

Tyre

SYRIA

PHOENICIA

724-722 B.C.

Sea of
Chinnereth

GALILEE

GILEAD

ISRAEL

701 B.C.

Samaria

Mt. Gerizim

FALL OF DAMASCUS
AND SAMARIA

0   50

Miles

Snow caps
Mixed coniferous and broadleaf forest
Dry broadleaf forest
Dry grassland
Desert grass and shrub
Barren deserts and mountains
Cropland, pastures, oases
Marsh

Jerusalem

JUDAH

Dead
Sea

© Copyright 1957 by Map Projects Inc.

rid of Ahab's seventy sons and the old queen, Jezebel. He slew forty-two princes of the house of David who were in Jezreel on a royal visit. He also massacred many worshipers of Baal.

Jehu tried to buy Assyria's help against the Syrians of Damascus by offering the Assyrian emperor, Shalmaneser III, a large amount of gold. This move was useless, however, for Hazael of Damascus continued to fight against Israel. By the end of his reign, Jehu had lost to the Syrians all of Gilead and Manasseh.

Under Jehu's son, Jehoahaz, Israel was practically a colony of Damascus. However, the Assyrians began to threaten the West again, and Damascus had to ease her rule. Jehoash of Israel (801–786 B.C.) even grew strong enough to reconquer some of the towns lost by Jehu.

QUEEN ATHALIAH OF JUDAH

Shortly after Jehu's revolution in Israel, a counter-revolution took place in Judah. Athaliah, a daughter of Ahab and Jezebel, had married Jehoram, king of Judah. When her son Ahaziah, who had succeeded Jehoram, was slain in Jehu's uprising in 842, Athaliah promptly murdered the rest of her family and seized the royal power for herself. She reigned in Judah for six years, until the priests brought out of hiding her little grandson Joash, whom they had rescued. The pagan idolatress Athaliah was put to death, and Joash became king, to reign until 800 B.C.

For a few years after the death of Joash, the kings of Judah and Israel still fought each other. Gradually the quarreling died down, however, and once more there was peace between the two sections of the country.

THE PROPHET AMOS

Except for minor troubles, peace reigned in the Fertile Crescent for more than fifty years, from about 800 to 745 B.C. In a new balance of power, Assyria was strong enough to keep Damascus from threatening Israel, but not strong enough to embark upon conquest herself. From the other direction, Egypt was not strong enough to interfere.

Tiglath-pileser III, the Assyrian king who conquered Israel.

By 745 B.C., under Tiglath-pileser III, the Assyrians were on the march again. Israel was panic-stricken. A wave of political violence brought Menahem (745–738 B.C.) to the Israelite throne. In 740 B.C. the Assyrian armies began to push south, and Arpad and Hamath fell. Menahem staved off an invasion by paying Tiglath-pileser a large sum of gold.

The political murders in Israel continued. Menahem's son was overthrown. During these troubled years, Israel tried in vain to find allies. The prophet Hosea called his nation a "dove, silly and without sense, calling to Egypt, going to Assyria." Like Amos, Hosea predicted the end of the kingdom of Israel.

THE PROPHET ISAIAH

A third voice joined the prophetic chorus—this time in Judah. When King Uzziah died (about 742 B.C.), a prince of the house of David, named Isaiah, had a vision of Yahweh in the temple of Jerusalem. Though Isaiah was not a poor shepherd like Amos, nor a small farmer like Hosea, he, too, spoke out against the social injustice and corruption of his day.

One of Isaiah's ideas proved to be very important to both Judaism and Christianity. He believed that though Israel and Judah would be destroyed, a "remnant" would repent and live.

Under the forty-year reign of King Jeroboam II (until 746 B.C.), Israel began to prosper. International trade restored some of the wealth of Omri and Ahab. People began to feel that happier times were ahead.

And so nobody believed the prophet Amos when he announced at Bethel in 751 B.C. that Israel would soon be destroyed. Amos was a poor shepherd from Tekoa in southern Judah. Like the prophet Elijah, he wanted social justice. Looking at the evil and greed in Israelite society, he did not think that God would long endure it.

An alabaster carving of the Assyrian king Ashurnasirpal hunting lions.

To make Jerusalem ready for a siege, Hezekiah, the son of Ahaz, had a tunnel dug so that the water of Gihon could flow underneath the city to the well-protected pool of Siloam.

In 735 B.C. young Ahaz came to the throne of Judah. Ahaz was badly frightened when King Pekah of Israel and King Rezin of Damascus tried to force him into a war against the mighty Assyrian emperor. Feverishly he prepared for a siege of the capital. As he was inspecting the water-supply near the spring of Gihon, Isaiah approached him with some good advice. The advice was to have faith in Yahweh and not to become fainthearted because of those two "smoking sticks," Pekah and Rezin.

But Ahaz would not listen. He was foolish enough to ask Tiglath-pileser for protection. Tiglath-pileser came and took Damascus in 732 B.C. after a two-year siege. He also captured the Israelite Galilee and Transjordan. The inhabitants of these regions were brutally marched into captivity a thousand miles away.

THE END OF ISRAEL

Tiglath-pileser replaced King Pekah of Israel with a puppet king he thought he could trust. This was Hoshea, who became the last king of Israel (732–724 B.C.).

But when Tiglath-pileser died, Hoshea plotted with Egypt against Tiglath-pileser's successor. The new emperor lost no time. Samaria was besieged, and after three long years it had to yield, in 722 B.C. Under the Assyrian Sargon II, the whole population of Israel was sent to other parts of the Assyrian empire. In this great move the Israelites (sometimes called the "Ten Lost Tribes") disappeared completely from history.

In their place, Sargon settled some of his war veterans and other peoples from the northeast. These became the ancestors of the Samaritans. A few Samaritans are still living today around Mount Gerizim, near the site of Shechem.

THE SURVIVAL OF JUDAH

After the end of Israel, the kingdom of Judah remained officially independent, but Ahaz had to pay a yearly tax to the Assyrian emperor. Ahaz's son Hezekiah (715-687 B.C.), however, joined in a general revolt.

Sennacherib, the Assyrian emperor who succeeded Sargon in 705 B.C., firmly put down the revolt. He overran the country, took forty-six fortified towns, and in 701 B.C. besieged Jerusalem. Plague broke out among his soldiers and forced him to retreat. But he had already made Hezekiah give up all his treasures—gold and silver, ivory beds and chairs, elephant skins, even his daughters and the women of the palace.

When Jerusalem was so unexpectedly saved, the aged Isaiah began to feel that after all the city would not perish, but remain the center of his people's faith. He also began to look forward to the time when "the wolf would dwell with the lamb," and

*"Nation shall not lift up sword against nation,
Neither shall they learn war any more."*

But Isaiah's prophecy of peace was still no more than a dream. With Esarhaddon (681–669 B.C.) and Asshurbanipal, who died in 630 B.C., the Assyrian empire reached the height of its military power and glory. From their sumptuous capital of Nineveh, the Assyrian emperors controlled the ancient world. Two kings of Judah, Manasseh and his son Amon, had to worship the Assyrian gods in the temple of Yahweh itself.

In those dark days the prophet Micah (about 701–650 B.C.), from Moresheth in Judah, kept on predicting the complete destruction of Jerusalem and of the temple. Less than seventy-five years later, Micah's words were to come true.

THE BABYLONIAN EMPIRE AND THE EXILE OF JUDAH

605–538 B.C.

*II Kings 22-25, Nahum 1-3, Zephaniah 1-3,
Habakkuk 1-3, Jeremiah 1-52, Lamentations 1-5,
Psalm 137, Ezekiel 1-48, Isaiah 40-55, The Book of Job*

THE POWER of Assyria waned. New peoples, the Scythians and the Medes, pushed in from the north and east, and the Babylonians from the south. In 612 B.C. Nineveh, proud Assyrian capital, fell. The prophet Nahum, in Judah, saw this as a sign of God's avenging justice.

Josiah was king in Jerusalem during these stirring times. Even before Nineveh fell, an old book of Yahweh's law for his people had been found in the temple. At once, King Josiah began a religious reform. He swept the Assyrian idols out of Jerusalem and destroyed pagan shrines in other cities. Henceforth the temple of Jerusalem was the only center of worship in Judah.

THE BATTLE OF CARCHEMISH, 605 B.C.

Unfortunately, the fall of Nineveh did not mean freedom for Judah; it meant the rule of Egypt. With Assyria out of the way, the Pharaoh Neco saw his chance.

Promptly he marched into Palestine, toward

Babylon was rebuilt by Nebuchadnezzar. One of its glories was the great Ishtar Gate, which led to the city's processional street.

Syria. King Josiah fought bravely against Neco's army at Megiddo (609 B.C.), but was slain there. His son Jehoahaz was carried off to Egypt in chains, and another son, Jehoiakim, was put on the throne of Judah.

However, the Babylonians were not willing to let the Egyptians capture the Fertile Crescent. In 605 B.C., Nebuchadnezzar defeated Neco at Carchemish. Babylon thus took the place of Nineveh as capital of the Near East.

When King Jehoiakim foolishly tried to revolt, however, hoping for help from Egypt, Nebuchadnezzar marched on Jerusalem, Jehoiakim was slain by his own men. Nebuchadnezzar took the king's son Jehoiachin (sometimes called Coniah) off to Babylon. Along with Coniah, Nebuchadnezzar took the royal treasures, the princes, the priests, the officers and craftsmen, and the upper classes of Judean society. They were marched in chains to Babylon, a thousand miles away. A third son of Josiah, named Zedekiah, was left on the throne of Judah (597–586 B.C.). He was merely a puppet, under the control of Babylon.

In Jerusalem the prophet Jeremiah watched with horror the death of his nation. Jeremiah saw clearly how tiny Judah was caught between strong Egypt and Babylon. But in spite of all of Jeremiah's warnings, King Zedekiah also tried to revolt.

This time the punishment was completely thorough. Nebuchadnezzar first burned to the ground all the fortresses of Judah, so completely that many were never rebuilt. Then he laid siege to Jerusalem. In 586 B.C. the city fell. The walls and palaces were destroyed and the temple was burned.

King Zedekiah's sons were slain before his eyes; then he was blinded and taken to Babylon in chains. The rest of the population—all except for a few of the poorest people—were taken with him. The prophets' words were finally fulfilled. The kingdom of David and Solomon had come to an end.

THE PROPHETS AND THE FAITH

At this point in their history, the people of Judah could simply have disappeared, like the Israelites. Instead, they became the Jews. Without a land, without a king, without a temple, they managed to stay together and heroically to keep their faith alive. They learned how to form a "congregation" even in a hostile land. Much of their courage came from the prophets.

Soon after King Coniah and the other exiles were taken to Babylon, Jeremiah sent them a letter. He said the exile would last a long time, and he advised them to adopt Babylonia as their home.

After the final destruction of Jerusalem, Jeremiah tried to remain in Judah. But the times were too troubled, and in 581 B.C. his friends took him to Egypt, where a number of Jews had fled. In Egypt, however, the Jews kept their faith less firmly than the Jews in Babylonia.

Before Jeremiah died, he announced that God would make a new covenant with the people of Israel to replace the old one, which they had broken.

Jeremiah's disciple and successor, Ezekiel, had been taken to Babylon with the first exiles. Like Jeremiah, he encouragingly preached that God would not abandon his people. He predicted they would return to their own land.

After a few years, the Jewish exiles were not too badly treated. In fact, Evil-merodach, the son of Nebuchadnezzar, rescued Coniah from prison and allowed him to live at court.

The nameless poet and prophet known as "Second Isaiah" (*Isaiah*, Chapters 40 to 55) understood that Israel had become a spiritual "church" rather than a political nationality. He proclaimed that its mission was to be "a light for the nations." He saw also that Babylonia was declining (about 545 B.C.). In the east, he hailed the Persian, Cyrus, as the "messiah" of Yahweh who would bring freedom to the Jews.

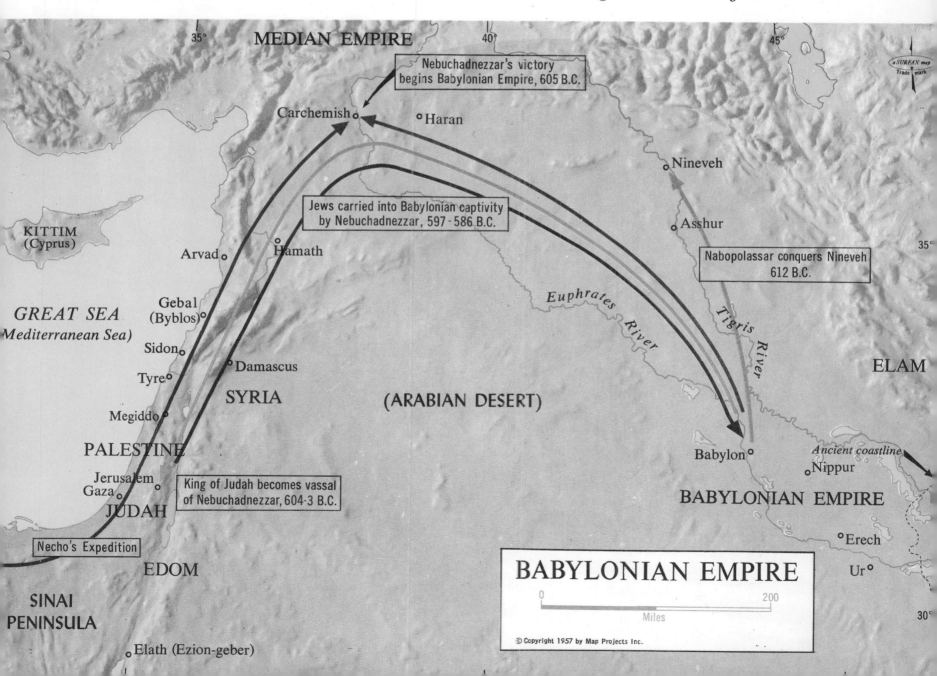

MEDIAN EMPIRE

Nebuchadnezzar's victory begins Babylonian Empire, 605 B.C.

Carchemish ° Haran

° Nineveh

Jews carried into Babylonian captivity by Nebuchadnezzar, 597-586 B.C.

° Asshur

Nabopolassar conquers Nineveh 612 B.C.

KITTIM (Cyprus)

Arvad ° ° Hamath

Euphrates River

Tigris River

GREAT SEA (Mediterranean Sea)

Gebal (Byblos) °

Sidon °

Tyre ° ° Damascus

ELAM

SYRIA (ARABIAN DESERT)

Megiddo °

PALESTINE

Babylon ° *Ancient coastline*

° Nippur

Jerusalem °
Gaza °

King of Judah becomes vassal of Nebuchadnezzar, 604-3 B.C.

JUDAH

BABYLONIAN EMPIRE

Necho's Expedition

EDOM

° Erech

BABYLONIAN EMPIRE

SINAI PENINSULA

Ur °

0 — 200
Miles

° Elath (Ezion-geber)

The Torah

THE PERSIAN EMPIRE
AND THE RESTORATION

539–333 B.C.

Ezra 1-10, Nehemiah 1-13, Haggai 1-2,
Zechariah 1-8, Joel, Malachi, Isaiah 56-66, Proverbs,
Song of Songs, Ruth, Jonah

AS THE prophet called the "Second Isaiah" had foreseen, King Cyrus of Persia was to be the next great master of the world. In 550 B.C., he defeated the Medes. In 539 B.C., Babylon fell into his hands. Almost at once he offered the Jews their freedom, along with the other enslaved populations of Babylonia.

The Persian empire was quite different from that of the Assyrians and Babylonians. Instead of leading nations off into captivity, the Persians allowed their subjects a great deal of freedom. Under a Persian governor, each region kept its own customs and religion, and managed many of its own affairs.

Before many years had passed, the Persian empire became the largest the world had ever seen. It stretched from the borders of India, in Asia, to Thrace, in Europe. The Greek states were

Persepolis, which lay on a great plain, was constructed on a platform made from the limestone of nearby mountains. One of its most beautiful buildings was the apadana, or audience hall. On its eastern staircase are carved Persian guards.

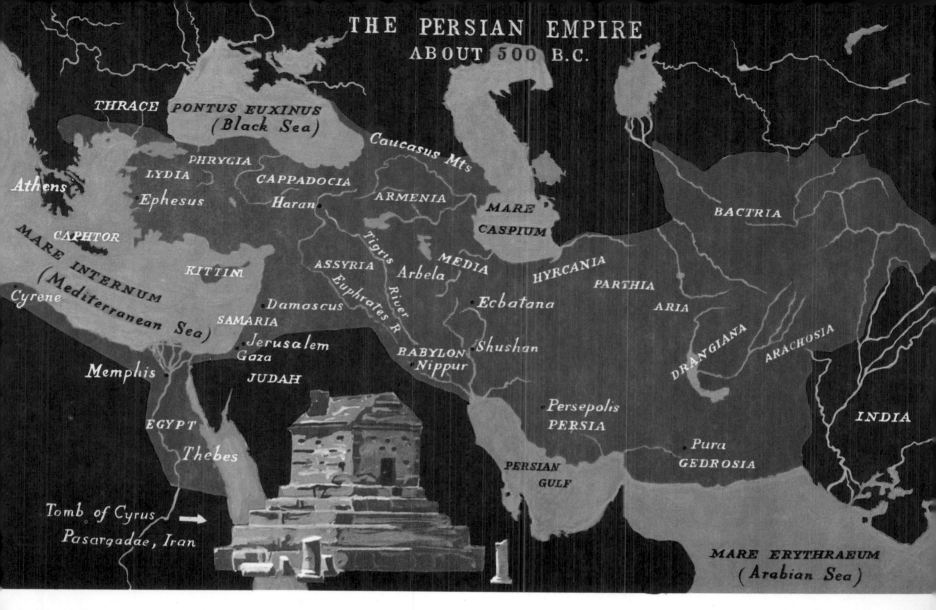

THRACE PONTUS EUXINUS (Black Sea)

Caucasus Mts

PHRYGIA

LYDIA CAPPADOCIA

Athens

Ephesus Haran ARMENIA

MARE CASPIUM

BACTRIA

CAPHTOR

MARE INTERNUM

KITTIM

ASSYRIA Arbela MEDIA

HYRCANIA

PARTHIA

(Mediterranean Sea)

Cyrene

Tigris River

Euphrates R.

Damascus

Ecbatana

ARIA

DRANGIANA

ARACHOSIA

SAMARIA

Jerusalem Gaza

BABYLON Shushan

Nippur

JUDAH

INDIA

Memphis

EGYPT

Thebes

Persepolis PERSIA

Pura GEDROSIA

Tomb of Cyrus
Pasargadae, Iran

PERSIAN GULF

MARE ERYTHRAEUM
(Arabian Sea)

threatened; even Egypt and Libya in Africa were under Persian rule. At home in Persia, the successors of Cyrus built many splendid palaces and public monuments, especially at Susa and Persepolis.

THE RETURN TO JUDAH

Not many of the Jews took advantage of Cyrus' offer to go back to the land of Judah. A mere handful of priests and their families returned to the ruins of Jerusalem. Most of the exiles preferred to stay in Mesopotamia, where they had farms and places of business.

Nor were the Jews welcomed to Judah when they got there. Samaritans, Edomites, Moabites, Ammonites, and Arabs had come in and settled the land. The Jewish community was poor. It was hard for the prophets Haggai and Zechariah to get the people interested in rebuilding the temple, as the center of Jewish religious life.

There was political unrest as well. After the death of Cambyses II of Persia in 522 B.C., several provinces of the empire tried to revolt.

Some of the Jews thought that the new governor of Judah, Zerubbabel, should declare himself king and proclaim Judah's independence. Fortunately, others in Jerusalem did not agree. Under the new emperor, Darius I, the temple was finally completed, in 516 B.C. It was small and drab, however—nothing like the splendid temple of Solomon.

NEHEMIAH AND EZRA

Over three-quarters of a century from the time the Jews returned from Babylon, the walls of Jerusalem were still in ruins, and the city open to attack. But Nehemiah, a high official at the Persian emperor's court, finally obtained his master's permission to go to Jerusalem and rebuild the walls.

In spite of the efforts of Sanballat, the governor of Samaria, to stop him, Nehemiah completed his task (445-443 B.C.). Often, half the people worked on the walls while the other half stood on guard, with weapons in their hands, to protect the workers.

Lion attacking a bull. A detail from the apadana at Persepolis.

A few years earlier, Artaxerxes I of Persia had allowed the "scribe" (scholar) Ezra to visit Jerusalem. Ezra was learned in the Law (the Torah), and helped to reorganize the religious life of the people.

Several years later, while on a second trip to Jerusalem, Ezra read publicly to all the people the five books of the Law. These five books, *Genesis* to *Deuteronomy,* are often called the Pentateuch ("five scrolls"). This event took place in the year 397 B.C.

More than any other one man, Ezra helped to make Judaism into the religion of the Law. To keep the Jewish faith pure, he set himself against marriage of Jews to foreigners. He even forced many of the men of Jerusalem to divorce their foreign wives.

JOEL AND MALACHI; THE JEWISH DISPERSION

The prophet Joel (about 400 B.C.) attempted to reform the lives of the priests, and urged all men to lead better lives.

The prophet Malachi, who lived about the same time, found Ezra too strict. He spoke against men divorcing their wives, even foreign ones. He believed that men would soon worship the Lord all over the world, "from the rising of the sun to the setting of the same."

Indeed, while Jerusalem was being rebuilt and Judaism established there, something equally important had been going on elsewhere. This was the Dispersion, or the establishment of prosperous Jewish communities throughout the Persian empire.

One center of the Jewish life was Elephantine in Egypt, near the First Cataract of the Nile. Another was Nippur, in Mesopotamia. These Jewish communities and others like them played an important part in Persian commerce and public life, as the story of Esther suggests. The Jews also carried their religion with them. Now it was no longer the religion of a small country. It had spread to many other parts of the world.

Aristotle

THE GREEK EMPIRE AND THE MACCABEES

333–63 B.C.

Ecclesiastes, I and II Maccabees, Daniel, Zechariah, 9–14

Alexander

AFTER two hundred years, the Persian Empire became weak in its turn. Under Artaxerxes III and Darius III (358 to 331 B.C.) it started falling apart. For the first time in history, the new master of Asia came out of Europe. He was Alexander of Macedon, a next-door neighbor to the Greeks.

Along with Alexander, Greek thought and civilization conquered Egypt, Mesopotamia, and the Fertile Crescent. The Greek language, art, and literature became strong influences in the Near East for the next few centuries—a fact which explains how the New Testament came to be written in Greek.

ALEXANDER THE GREAT, 336–323 B.C.

As the pupil of the philosopher and scientist Aristotle, Alexander had one of the best Greek educations of his day. At the age of twenty-one, this handsome and brilliant youth was ready to conquer the world.

He began by defeating Darius III at Issus in Asia Minor. Then, moving swiftly southward, he took Damascus, Sidon, Tyre, and (in 333 B.C.) Jerusalem.

According to legend, Alexander was so impressed by a procession of priests from the temple that he did not destroy Jerusalem. He also allowed the Jews to follow their special customs.

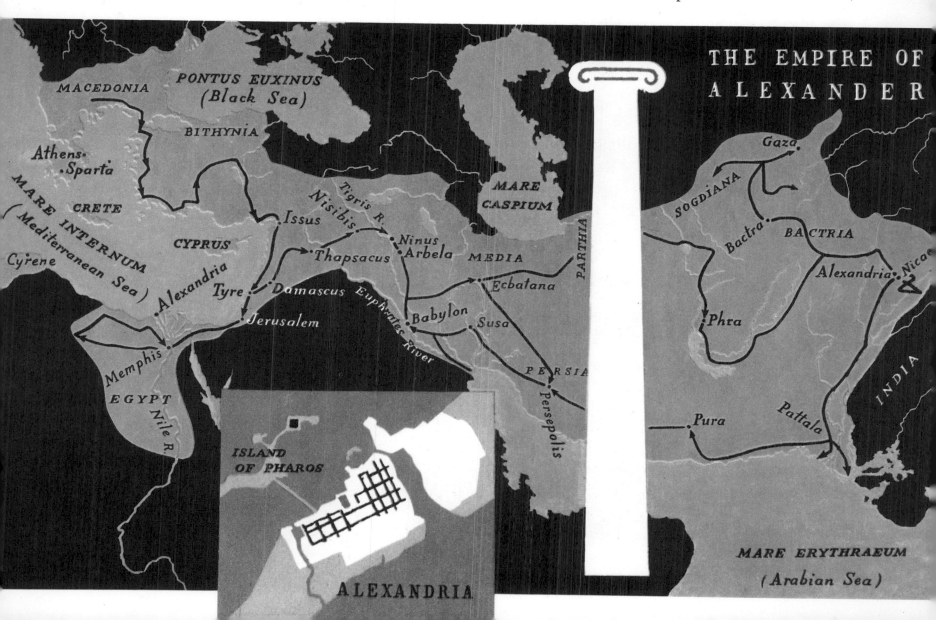
THE EMPIRE OF ALEXANDER

From Jerusalem, Alexander went on to conquer Egypt, and established the city of Alexandria in the Nile Delta. Striking northward again, he defeated Darius III near Arbela (330 B.C.). The Persian Empire was now his: he seized Babylon, Susa, and Persepolis. After a long campaign to the very borders of India, he returned to Babylon and died at the age of thirty-three.

THE PTOLEMIES, THE SELEUCIDS, AND THE JEWS

Immediately, Alexander's generals began to fight among themselves for his empire. A general named Ptolemy seized Egypt, and another general named Seleucus finally established himself at Antioch in North Syria. Five Ptolemies reigned in Egypt from 323 to 181 B.C. During much of this period, Palestine was under Egyptian rule.

However, the Seleucids (descendants of Seleucus) in Syria also wished to control Palestine. From 300 to 200 B.C. it was often a battleground between the two rival dynasties. In 198 B.C. the Seleucids finally won out and gained control of Jerusalem. For thirty years, however, they allowed the Jews to live and worship as they pleased.

The Ptolemies and the Seleucids were both Hellenistic—that is, Greek in their culture. Greek thinking and Greek ways of life affected even the Jews. Many Jews wore the Greek dress, attended Greek games and plays, and adopted Greek architecture and customs. Alexandria, in Egypt, had become a great center of Greek thought, and a number of Jews settled there. These Greek-speaking Jews no longer understood the books of the Law and the Prophets in the original Hebrew, and the sacred writings were translated into Greek. This Greek translation, called the Septuagint, was later taken over by the early Christians.

THE MACCABEAN WAR, 167–160 B.C.

Hellenized as many Jews had become, they were still Jews in their religion. A Seleucid ruler, Antiochus Epiphanes, set out to change this. Using as an excuse a quarrel between two rival high priests, he ordered the Jews to worship the Greek gods. He himself profaned the temple of Jerusalem in 167 B.C. by offering there a swine to the Olympian Zeus. All through Palestine, altars to the gods were set up, and the Jews were forced to sacrifice at them.

But at the little town of Modein, the aged priest Mattathias refused to sacrifice to the heathen gods. He slew the Syrian officer, and with his five sons escaped to the hills. Soon many other people joined them.

Judas Maccabee ("Judas the Hammerer"), son of Mattathias, became the leader. He and his small band of heroic fighters succeeded in driv-

Pharos, an off-shore island at Alexandria, was connected with the mainland by Alexander the Great. On Pharos stood a great lighthouse, one of the seven wonders of the ancient world.

58

Maccabean coins.

ing the trained army of Antiochus out of Jerusalem. On December 25, 164 B.C., Judas was able to purify the temple and restore worship there. This event is still remembered in the feast of Hanukkah.

THE HASMONEAN DYNASTY, 160–63 B.C.

Two brothers of Judas Maccabee, Jonathan and Simon, finally won the independence of Palestine. Thus was founded the "Hasmonean dynasty," named from Hashmon, the Maccabees' ancestor. The Hasmoneans were both high priests and kings. Jonathan was later captured and killed by the Syrians and Simon was murdered by his son-in-law. But Simon's son John Hyrcanus settled down to a successful reign of thirty years (134–104 B.C.).

Hyrcanus gained control of Samaria and of the plain of Jezreel. He destroyed the Samaritan temple on Mount Gerizim, rival of the temple in Jerusalem. Under his sons, Aristobulus I and Alexander Jannaeus, the kingdom grew even larger.

However, some of the Jews began to turn against the Maccabean kings, who were more interested in war and conquest than in religion. Finally, quarrels broke out in the royal family itself. Two sons of Alexander Jannaeus, Hyrcanus II and Aristobulus II, fought each other for the kingdom. Antipater, governor of Idumea (Edom) to the south, saw a chance to stir up trouble, and sided with Hyrcanus. Hyrcanus appealed to the Roman general Pompey.

It was just the kind of situation which the Romans, the new masters of the world, were waiting for. In 63 B.C. the great Roman general Pompey entered Jerusalem.

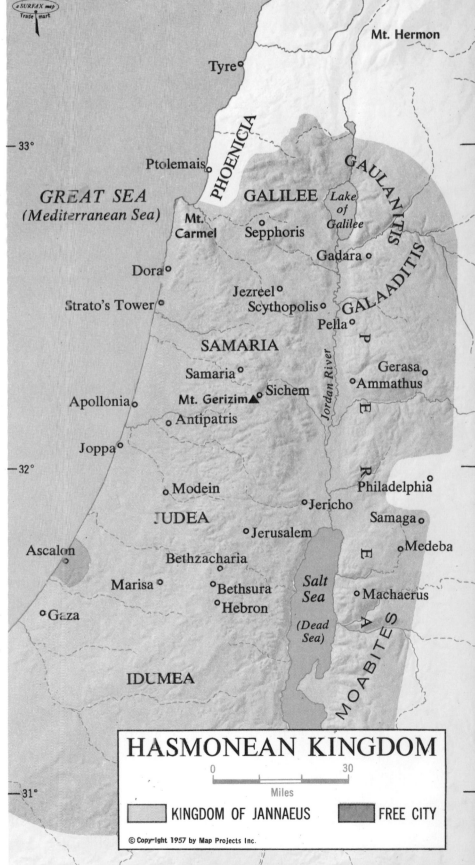

HASMONEAN KINGDOM

0   30
Miles

KINGDOM OF JANNAEUS   FREE CITY

© Copyright 1957 by Map Projects Inc.

Roman eagle

THE ROMAN CONQUEST AND THE BIRTH OF JESUS

63 B.C.–A.D. 14

Matthew 1–2, Luke 1–2

LIKE THE Greeks, the new conquerors of Palestine were Europeans. With the coming of the Romans, the center of the world moved westward to Italy.

Though Rome had begun as a city-state and a republic, for many years it had owned colonies all around the Mediterranean. Pompey, a Roman general, came to the Near East to gain control of that area for Rome. When Pompey entered Jerusalem in 63 B.C., the independence of Palestine was over.

THE ROMAN EMPIRE AND KING HEROD

Pompey captured Aristobulus and shocked the Jews by lifting the curtain before the Holy of Holies in the temple. Hyrcanus II became the high priest, but the real power was in the hands of Antipater, an Idumean (Edomite). Antipater was hated by the Jews; in 43 B.C. he was poisoned. The Parthians, an eastern people who had not submitted to Rome, took this opportunity to seize Jerusalem. Antigonus, the son of Aristobulus, who had invited their help, was put on the throne.

During these years, the Roman Republic became an empire. Pompey was defeated by the brilliant general Julius Caesar, who was himself assassinated in 44 B.C. Then the struggle for power was between Octavius, youthful grand-nephew of Julius Caesar, and the general Mark Antony. Antony allied himself with Cleopatra, the intelligent and attractive queen of Egypt. Formerly her charms had captivated the aging

60

OCEANUS ATLANTICUS
(Atlantic Ocean)

40°

LUSITANIA

TARRACONENSIS

°Tarraco

BAETICA

°Carthago Nova

MAURETANIA

30°

0°

AQUITANIA

NAR

R
ITS EXTE
BIRTH

0

© Copyright 1957 by Map Projects Inc.

Julius Caesar, and now she was the friend and ally of Antony. At the naval battle of Actium (31 B.C.), Antony and Cleopatra were defeated and fled to their death in Alexandria. Octavius, taking the name of Caesar Augustus, became the ruler of the world.

In the meantime, the Roman government had appointed Herod, the son of Antipater, to be "king of the Jews." With Roman soldiers from Syria, the new king captured Jerusalem. But he did not have an easy time. The Jews hated him, even though he tried to gain their friendship by marrying a Hasmonean princess, Mariamne. Cleopatra, too, plotted against him, and he was saved from ruin only by her death.

ELGICA

RAETIA

NORICUM

ALPS

PANNONIA

DACIA

PONTUS EUXINUS
(Black Sea)

ILLYRICUM

Danube R.

Mare Hadriaticum

MOESIA

THRACIA

Byzantium

BITHYNIA ET PONTUS

GALATIA

CAPPADOCIA

MACEDONIA

Thessalonica

Mare Aegaeum

Pergamum

ASIA

Smyrna

Ephesus

Miletus

CILICIA ET SYRIA

Tarsus

CORSICA
ET
SARDINIA

Rome

Ostia

ITALIA

Mare Tyrrhenum

ACHAIA

Actium

Athenae

Corinthus

LYCIA

Rhegium

SICILIA

Sparta

Rhodes

RHODES

CYPRUS

Damascus

Carthage

Mediterranean Sea

INTERNUM

Cnossus

CRETA

MARE

(Mediterranean Sea)

ME
AT THE
JESUS

300

roads

sea routes

Nazareth

Caesarea

Sebaste

Jerusalem

Bethlehem

AFRICA

CYRENAICA

AEGYPTUS

Alexandria

Memphis

10°   20°   30°

Pompey the Great

Julius Caesar

Emperor Augustus

Mark Antony

Cleopatra

61

In many parts of the world the Romans built large cities with columned forums, temples, theaters, aqueducts, and public baths for the housing and comfort of their legionnaires. Still standing in the orange and pink granite city of Gerasa are a large theater and a small one, many temples, and a great processional street with more than one hundred columns.

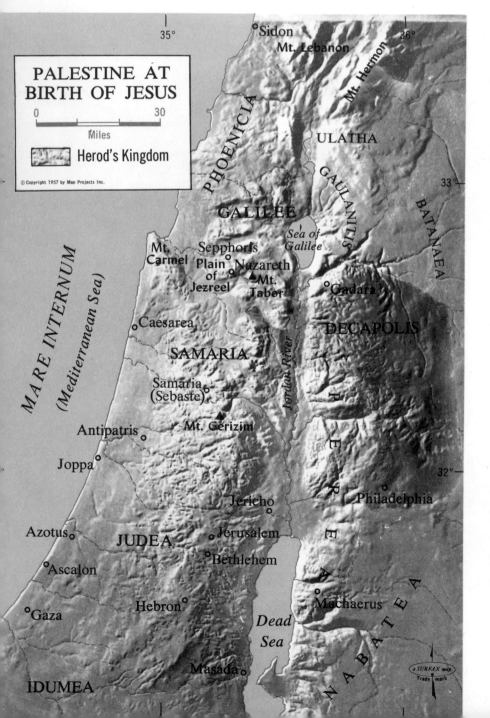

PALESTINE AT
BIRTH OF JESUS

0   30
Miles

Herod's Kingdom

© Copyright 1957 by Map Projects Inc.

Herod was a pagan by birth and culture. He put up shrines to his master Augustus, who was worshiped as a god throughout the empire. He rebuilt, in the Greek style, the new city of Samaria (Sebaste) and the harbor town of Caesarea.

But Herod respected the religion of the Jews. He rebuilt the temple on a magnificent scale, with vast courtyards, terraces, and porticoes. He also rebuilt and extended the ancient aqueducts which brought water to Jerusalem from Wadi Urtas, near the Pools of Solomon.

BIRTH OF JESUS

According to the gospels, Jesus was born in Bethlehem just before Herod's death in 4 B.C. There is a mistake in our calendar; the true date of Jesus' birth is probably near 6 B.C. The story of the massacre of the Bethlehem children at the time of Jesus is true to the character of the aged king. All his life, Herod feared conspiracy; as he grew old, he became an insane murderer. He killed most of his relatives, including three of his own sons.

THE ROMAN WORLD IN THE TIME OF JESUS

The Roman emperor Caesar Augustus or Octavius, was an excellent organizer. He established the subject states and kingdoms as provinces of the Roman Empire, ruled by puppet kings or Roman public servants called "procurators." A great network of hard-surfaced roads was begun. On these roads, Roman soldiers could quickly travel everywhere, to keep order. The Roman army was organized into well-armed and splendidly disciplined "legions." The *Pax Romana* ("Roman peace") they enforced made the lands and seaways of the Mediterranean safe for travelers and goods.

The Roman culture was similar to the Greek culture which had spread all through the Fertile Crescent. In Transjordan was the Decapolis, a league of the Greek cities that had grown up in the past two hundred years. East and south of the Decapolis were the Parthians and the Nabateans, peoples still unfriendly to Rome. As a result, the Romans were deeply interested in Palestine, and kept strict control of its affairs.

JEWISH RELIGIOUS GROUPS

The Jews felt threatened by this pagan culture pressing in on them. Time and time again they revolted, and the cruelty with which the revolts were crushed made them hate the Romans even more. For example, about the time Jesus was born some Jews tore down the Roman golden eagle which stood at the gates of the temple. They were condemned to be burned alive, and an angry mob stoned the Roman legionnaires. To put down the riots which followed, the Roman general Varus crucified two thousand patriots. Their bodies were left hanging on the crosses for days, along the road from Jerusalem to Galilee. Similar sights must have been seen by the boy Jesus as he traveled with his family.

All the Jews hated Rome, but the different classes of society acted in different ways. The wealthy Sadducees, friends of the high priests, collaborated with the Romans. They did so to protect their wealth and their control of the Jewish council called the Sanhedrin, which still had some power.

The Pharisees and the learned Scribes did not collaborate with the Romans. They withdrew from public affairs and became extremely religious. Other religious sects, like the Essenes, withdrew from society altogether, and practiced their religion in monasteries. An important monastery was recently discovered at Khirbet Qumran, near the Dead Sea.

The Zealots, mostly Jews of the Galilean hills, wanted to make open war against Rome. They welcomed, one after another, more than a dozen leaders who claimed to be the "Messiah," or the "Anointed One"—a descendant of David who would bring about the Kingdom of God. All these men were killed by the Roman authorities.

The desert of Judah. This is the "wilderness" in which John the Baptist preached.

63

The town of Nazareth, childhood home of Jesus, as seen a few years ago.

The common people—the peasants, the shepherds, the laborers, the carpenters, the smiths—hesitated between the teachings of the Pharisees and the wild dreams of the Zealots. They went to the local synagogue, or house of prayer, every Sabbath. There they sang the Psalms, read the Scriptures, and waited for their deliverance.

Mary's Well, in Nazareth, the location of which has remained unchanged through the ages. It is the only ancient well in the town.

JESUS IN NAZARETH

It was among these poor, hard-working, bewildered and faithful folk that Jesus grew up. In the small town of Nazareth in Galilee, he learned the carpenter's trade, which meant the work of building houses in wood and stone.

From the hills overlooking the town, Jesus could see the fertile Plain of Jezreel, with Mount Carmel in the distance, and even glimpse the Mediterranean. He could go a few miles north of Nazareth to the pagan city of Sepphoris, where Greek was spoken instead of Aramaic, his native tongue. (Aramaic had become the language of trade and daily use throughout this region.)

From Mount Tabor, a few miles to the east, Jesus could look down on the deep Jordan Valley and see the Transjordan Plateau beyond. Here were the Greek cities of the Decapolis, with their temples, theaters, stadiums, and pagan ways.

In Nazareth, he could go to the synagogue and learn to read and write, as well as to sing and pray. Once a year or so, he would accompany Mary and Joseph and his brothers and sisters to Jerusalem, for the Passover. Here he became familiar with the temple in which, the gospel of Luke tells us, as a boy of twelve years, he was discovered by his family arguing with the teachers of the Law.

THE EARLY PREACHING OF JESUS

A.D. 27–28

Matthew 3–15, Mark 1–7, Luke 3–8, John 1–3

Galilean fishing boat

ACCORDING TO the gospel of Luke, Jesus began his public life in the fifteenth year of the reign of the Roman emperor Tiberius. This would have been A.D. 28, when Jesus was about thirty-two years old.

At this time, Palestine was divided into three districts, under three different rulers. Two of the rulers were sons of King Herod, and the third was a Roman procurator. During the ministry of Jesus, the procurator was a man named Pontius Pilate.

One of Herod's sons, Herod Antipas, was tetrarch (commander) of Galilee and Perea. He seems to have been weak and treacherous; Jesus called him "that fox." Philip, the other son, who ruled the region northeast of the Sea of Galilee, was considered honest and fair. The Greek cities of the Decapolis were in Transjordan and mainly governed themselves.

JESUS AND JOHN THE BAPTIST

The public life of Jesus falls into two main periods. During the early period, he spent most of his time in Galilee, where he began preaching soon after the appearance of John the Baptist.

John was a prophet in the tradition of Elijah. He may have been a friend of the Essenes, monks who lived near the Dead Sea. Like the prophets of old, John lived in the desert, ate locusts and wild honey, and wore a robe of camel's hair tied with a leather belt. He called on the people to repent, warning them that the Kingdom of God was near. Large crowds came down to the Jordan Valley to hear John preach. There, as a sign that they were cleansed from sin, that their past was dead and that they were reborn to a new life,

John baptized them in the waters of the Jordan.

For a time, Jesus seems to have been a follower of John. He came from Nazareth to hear John and be baptized, but left John soon afterwards. He withdrew into the "wilderness"—the

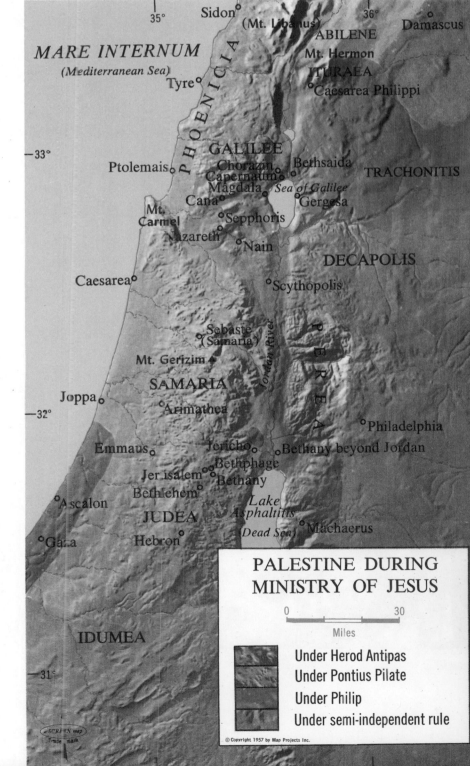

PALESTINE DURING MINISTRY OF JESUS

0   30

Miles

Under Herod Antipas
Under Pontius Pilate
Under Philip
Under semi-independent rule

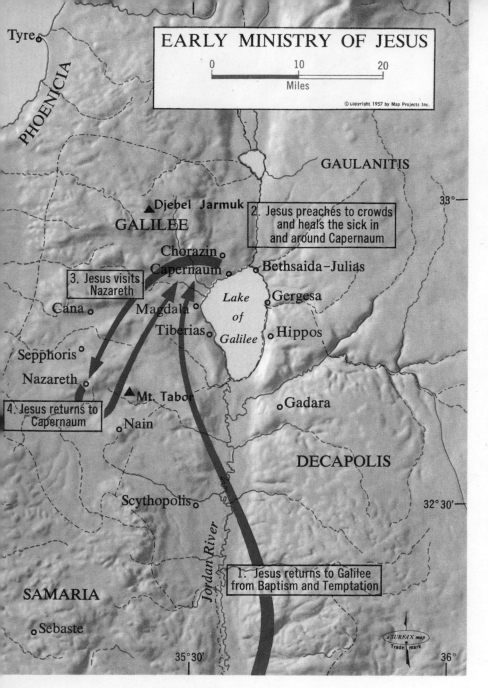

EARLY MINISTRY OF JESUS

0   10   20
Miles
© Copyright 1957 by Map Projects Inc.

PHOENICIA

Tyre

GAULANITIS

Djebel Jarmuk

GALILEE

2. Jesus preaches to crowds and heals the sick in and around Capernaum

Chorazin
Capernaum

Bethsaida–Julias

3. Jesus visits Nazareth

Cana

Magdala

Gergesa

Lake of Galilee

Tiberias

Hippos

Sepphoris

Nazareth

Mt. Tabor

4. Jesus returns to Capernaum

Nain

Gadara

DECAPOLIS

Scythopolis

Jordan River

1. Jesus returns to Galilee from Baptism and Temptation

SAMARIA

Sebaste

a SURFAX map
Trade mark

35°30'

36°

33°

32°30'

The Mount of Temptation is the modern name of a cliff at the edge of the Wilderness of Judea, overlooking the Jordan valley. According to tradition, Jesus spent 40 days there in fasting and prayer.

66

dreadful, barren hills around the Dead Sea—and lived there for forty days without food, in prayer and meditation. During this time, Jesus was tempted to follow the ideas of the Zealots. But he decided that military force could not deliver the Jews from Roman rule, and chose instead the weapons of humility and love.

JESUS IN CAPERNAUM

After his sojourn in the wilderness, Jesus began to preach. Like John, he announced that the Kingdom of God was at hand. Unlike John, however, he did not wait for people to come to him. He went to the towns and villages to give the people the good news—or gospel—of God's forgiveness and love.

Although the writers of the first three gospels —Mark, Matthew, and Luke—tell many of the same stories about Jesus, they do not give a clear picture of his travels. It is impossible to trace the routes he followed, or the order of the places he visited. Nevertheless, it seems clear that he began his public life in and around the town of Capernaum, on the northwestern shore of Lake Gennesaret in Galilee.

Capernaum stands on a small plain seven hundred feet below the level of the Mediterranean Sea; in the summer, it is extremely hot. In the time of Jesus, this plain was very fertile, but its swarms of flies and mosquitoes made it a breeding place for disease. Many people lived there, mostly poor farmhands who worked for a few wealthy landowners.

At Capernaum, Jesus went to the poor and the sick. He healed many of them, especially lepers and paralytics. Jesus did not try to gain the favor of the Sadducees or the Scribes and Pharisees. Instead, he made friends with tax collectors (known as "publicans"), fishermen, and people the Pharisees called "sinners." One of these was Mary Magdalene, who was a native of the town of Magdala. Some of these people, like the fishermen Simon Peter, Andrew, James, and John, became not only friends of Jesus but devoted followers.

The Sermon on the Mount was probably preached from the hills high above the town of

On the Sea of Galilee, also called Lake Tiberias, fishing boats similar to those used in the time of Jesus still ply the waters.

Capernaum. The multitudes who listened could look down at the beautiful lake with its boats, and see, beyond the lake, the brown and purple hills of Gerasa. To the northeast, at the water's edge, stood the town of Bethsaida; Chorazin nestled near by. In the springtime the hills of Galilee are covered with red anemones. Perhaps these were the "lilies of the field" which Jesus compared to Solomon arrayed in all his glory.

JESUS IN NAZARETH

After preaching in and near Capernaum, Jesus returned to his home town of Nazareth. There he was received again by his fellow towns-men not as a spiritual leader but as just the son of the local carpenter.

But Jesus now represented himself otherwise. One Sabbath, at the service in the synagogue, he read from the *Book of Isaiah,* and quoted the words of the prophet:

> *"The Spirit of the Lord is upon me
> Because he has anointed me to preach
> the good news to the poor."*

In the town of Capernaum, where Jesus preached on the shores of the Lake of Galilee, stand the partially restored ruins of a synagogue built after the time of Jesus.

This statement deeply shocked his listeners. To them the word "anointed" meant "the Anointed One," or Messiah, whose coming had for so long been foretold by the Hebrew prophets. It was unbelievable that this lowly young man could be the one chosen to lead the Hebrew people out of their troubles.

Then, by recalling Elijah, who had been sent to help a pagan woman rather than his fellow Israelites, Jesus hinted that it was not they whom he had come to save.

At once the shock of the people of Nazareth turned into rage.

An angry mob rushed Jesus out of Nazareth to a sharp cliff which overlooks the Plain of Es-draelon. They would gladly have thrown him over the cliff, but he escaped and returned to Capernaum. From this point on, Jesus was to meet increasing opposition to his teaching.

67

THE LATER PREACHING OF JESUS

A.D. 28–29

Matthew 16–20, Mark 8–13, Luke 9:1–19:27, John 4–11

The Lamb of God

Figs

FOR A WHILE, crowds flocked to hear Jesus preach. His early admirers even tried to crown him king, hoping that he would lead a revolt against Rome.

But Jesus often said and did strange things. He did not believe in observing some of the religious laws, such as those about the Sabbath, too strictly. He even healed the slave of a Roman officer. The people were confused and began to stay away from him. Only his little band of friends remained with him.

John the Baptist had been put in prison because he had spoken out against the tetrarch,

Jacob's Well, where Jesus on his way to Jerusalem may have talked about the water of life with the woman from Sychar, A.D. 28–29.

68

Herod Antipas. Now Jesus learned that John had been put to death, and that Herod's police also were looking for him. Leaving Galilee, Jesus went north to the region around Tyre and Sidon. Then he and his followers, or disciples, set out for the city of Caesarea Philippi, in Philip's territory, safely out of Herod's reach.

ON THE ROAD TO CAESAREA PHILIPPI

The turning point in Jesus' life came on the road to Caesarea Philippi. First he asked his disciples if they, too, meant to desert him. Then he suddenly asked, "Who do you think I am?" Peter answered, "Thou art the Messiah." (In Greek, the word for Messiah is "Christos," from which we get the English word "Christ.") From that moment, Jesus no longer tried to preach to the crowds.

Six days later, Jesus led three of his disciples, Peter, James, and John, up "a high mountain." Here, to their eyes, he suddenly appeared as if changed, or transfigured. His clothes shone glistening white, and the three disciples saw Elijah and Moses talking with him.

Christian tradition has placed this scene on Mount Tabor, which rises above the hills of southern Galilee and the Plain of Jezreel. It is possible, however, that the place was Mount Hermon, which is very near Caesarea Philippi. Mount Hermon is more than eight thousand feet high, and its summit is capped with snow. In that dazzling whiteness, Peter, James, and John understood that in choosing the path of suffering and death, Jesus was really showing them, in a new and revealing way, the God of Moses and Elijah, the God of "The Law" and "The Prophets."

IN JERUSALEM, A.D. 28

Toward the end of the year A.D. 28, Jesus went to Jerusalem. The journey took courage, for many prophets had been put to death in that city.

According to the gospel of John, Jesus spent some time in Jerusalem, where his preaching and healing of the sick started a great deal of argument. Some people thought he was a holy man, and others were sure he must be possessed by a demon. During the Feast of the Dedication (December 25) he spoke in one of the courts of the temple, and the people tried to stone him.

Like some of the prophets of old, Jesus foretold the destruction of the temple. When one of his disciples said, "Look, Master, what wonderful stones and buildings!" Jesus answered, "There will not be left here one stone upon another that will not be thrown down!"

IN PEREA AND THE WILDERNESS

Leaving Jerusalem, Jesus went across the Jordan to Perea. Here he stayed several weeks during the winter of A.D. 28–29. Most likely he lived with the small group of his faithful followers, teaching them privately about his coming suffering and death.

Later, Jesus went to a place called Ephraim in the wilderness of Judea, between Bethel and Jericho. In this stern land of rocky cliffs and deep ravines, he must have thought deeply about the meaning of his life and what he should do. He could give up his preaching and go back to Nazareth. He could remain in the wilderness. Or he could return to Jerusalem and almost certain death. He had made bitter enemies among the priests and the Sadducees, and the Romans were always fearful that some Jewish leader would start a political revolt.

When his plans were clearly made, Jesus went down once more to the valley of the Jordan. He started for Jerusalem, passing through Jericho.

The road from Jericho to Jerusalem wound steeply up to the top of the mountain range. A few miles below the summit, Jesus reached the village of Bethany. He probably stayed there for the night with friends. Then he made arrangements to enter Jerusalem.

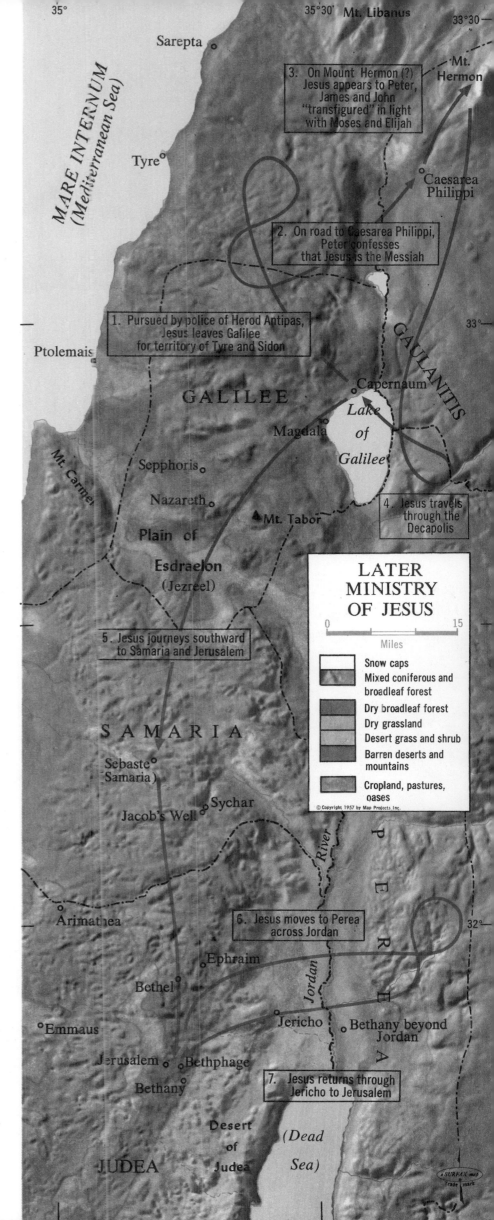

3. On Mount Hermon (?) Jesus appears to Peter, James and John "transfigured" in light with Moses and Elijah

2. On road to Caesarea Philippi, Peter confesses that Jesus is the Messiah

1. Pursued by police of Herod Antipas, Jesus leaves Galilee for territory of Tyre and Sidon

4. Jesus travels through the Decapolis

5. Jesus journeys southward to Samaria and Jerusalem

6. Jesus moves to Perea across Jordan

7. Jesus returns through Jericho to Jerusalem

LATER MINISTRY OF JESUS

0   Miles   15

Snow caps
Mixed coniferous and broadleaf forest
Dry broadleaf forest
Dry grassland
Desert grass and shrub
Barren deserts and mountains
Cropland, pastures, oases

© Copyright 1957 by Map Projects Inc.

Sheep and doves for sacrifice

THE DEATH OF JESUS

A.D. 29

Matthew 21–27, Mark 11–15,
Luke 19:28–23:56, John 12–19

IT WAS springtime, when the hills of the Judean wilderness are crimson with wild flowers. In a few more days the Jews would hold the feast of the Passover, to celebrate the escape from Egypt.

This was the season that Jesus chose for his triumphal entry into Jerusalem. His disciples found a donkey for him to ride. As the gospel of Matthew shows, this had a special meaning known to all the people watching the procession. The prophet Zechariah had foretold that the king would enter Jerusalem "humble, and mounted on a donkey." A military leader would have chosen to ride a horse. By choosing a donkey, Jesus was saying once again that his mission was one of peace and love.

His followers, and many of the onlookers, cut branches to strew on the road, crying,

"Hosannah to the Son of David!
Blessed be the King that cometh
in the name of the Lord!"

Some Pharisees asked Jesus to silence his disciples, but he refused. At that moment, he came to the top of the Mount of Olives, and the whole city of Jerusalem lay spread out at his feet. Looking at its walls and terraces, its towers and roofs, and the beautiful temple with its pillars and its porticoes, Jesus wept because he could not make the city understand his message of peace.

Modern Jerusalem as seen from Mount of Olives. The Dome of the Rock and the area where the temple stood are just below.

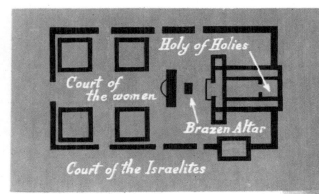

Entering Jerusalem, Jesus went straight to the courts of the temple. There, instead of proclaiming himself king, he drove out the money changers, the merchants who sold pigeons for the sacrifices, and the people who came to the temple to trade and chat instead of to worship. He reminded them of the words of the prophet Jeremiah, pronounced in the same spot six hundred years before:

"My house shall be called
A house of prayer for all the nations.
But you have made it a den of thieves."

A reconstruction of Herod's Temple. It stood on the site of the present-day mosque, Dome of the Rock.

Hearing this, the chief priests and the scribes who taught in the temple courts agreed that Jesus was a dangerous person. But they did not dare to have him arrested. They feared that the crowds of poor people, who admired Jesus, would rise up against them.

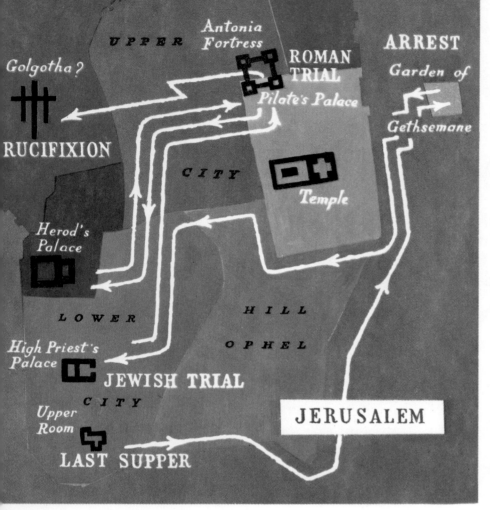

UPPER

Golgotha?

RUCIFIXION

Antonia
Fortress

ROMAN
TRIAL

Pilate's Palace

CITY

Temple

Herod's
Palace

LOWER

HILL

OPHEL

High Priest's
Palace

JEWISH TRIAL

CITY

Upper
Room

LAST SUPPER

ARREST

Garden of

Gethsemane

JERUSALEM

That night, and for several nights thereafter, Jesus went back to Bethany. During the day he was in Jerusalem, teaching in the temple. On Thursday night Jesus did not return to Bethany. He had his last meal with the disciples.

THE LAST NIGHT

The "last supper" was in the house of a friend who lived, according to a later tradition, in the southwestern quarter of the city. The meal was probably a Passover feast. If, in A.D. 29, the Passover began on Friday night, Galilean pilgrims had to return home before the Sabbath, on which day travel was forbidden, and so they were allowed to celebrate the feast a day early.

At any rate, Jesus gave to this meal a special meaning. By breaking bread and offering wine, he linked his coming death with the new covenant, or "testament," announced by the prophet Jeremiah at the time of the Babylonian exile.

After singing a psalm, Jesus and his disciples went across the Kidron Valley to the Mount of Olives. On the slope of the mountain was a small garden called Gethsemane ("the oil press").

72

From Gethsemane, Jesus could have climbed in a few minutes to the top of the mountain, and escaped to the east or south through the deep canyons of the Desert of Judea. Pursuers could scarcely have found him there.

But he did not choose to escape. He remained, praying, while Peter, James, and John fell fast asleep.

In Gethsemane, as he must have expected, Jesus was arrested. Judas Iscariot, one of the disciples, had arranged with the priests to betray Jesus. Now Judas arrived with a small detachment of the temple police, and perhaps some Roman soldiers.

The disciples woke up and fled. But the police led the unresisting Jesus to the house of the high priest Caiaphas, where members of the Jewish assembly, the Sanhedrin, were gathered. The Sanhedrin did not have the power to condemn to death. Its members simply declared Jesus guilty of a crime deserving death. Then they sent him off to Pontius Pilate, the Roman procurator.

The traditional Via Dolorosa, along which Jesus passed on his way to the hill of Golgotha, where he was crucified.

Learning that the accused man was a Galilean, Pilate sent him to Herod Antipas, the ruler of Galilee, who also happened to be in the city at the time. Antipas mocked Jesus, and tried vainly to question him. Finally he sent him back to Pilate, who ordered him crucified.

Archaeological excavations have uncovered, on the site of the Antonia Fortress, the actual pavement of the courtyard where the Roman soldiers of the guard kept their watch. To pass the time, they played what was called "the King's game," something like parcheesi. Lines for the game were scratched on the stones of the courtyard, in the very place where Jesus was whipped, mocked as king, and crowned with thorns.

When morning came, Jesus was marched to a hill called Golgotha (in Aramaic, "the skull"). There he was crucified with two thieves. Christian tradition places Golgotha at the site of the present Church of the Holy Sepulchre. However, in Jesus' time the city wall was probably west and north of this location; and if so, the exact place of the crucifixion is unknown. It is equally impossible to locate the tomb in the garden of Joseph of Arimathea, where the body of Jesus was laid to rest.

The Garden of Gethsemane, where Jesus was arrested.

Bush from which the crown of thorns may have been made.

The pavement of Antonia

A detail of the King's game on the paving stones

THE RESURRECTION AND THE EARLY CHURCH

A.D. 29–35

Matthew 28, Mark 16, Luke 24, John 20–21, Acts 1–8, 10

Symbol of bread

Symbol of wine

THE STORY of Jesus did not end with Golgotha. The gospels go on to relate that Jesus appeared to his followers after his death, but there are differences in the accounts as to the number of the appearances and the manner in which they occurred.

Since Jesus had died on Friday, just before the beginning of the Sabbath, no one could come on Saturday to embalm his body. But women who had been among his disciples came early Sunday morning, bringing the spices with them. The tomb was dug out of rock on a rocky slope; its door was a large, flat stone. As the women were wondering how they could move the heavy stone, they saw that it was already rolled away and that the tomb was empty. In a vision, an angel, or angels, told them that Jesus had risen from the dead and would see his disciples again in Galilee.

The gospels differ somewhat concerning the names of the women that went to the tomb. They also differ on whether they or Simon Peter first discovered that the body of Jesus was no longer there. According to the gospel of John, the only woman who visited the tomb was Mary Magdalene.

The gospels and the *Acts of the Apostles* do not agree on the number of times the friends of Jesus saw him. In the gospel of Matthew, the eleven disciples (Judas had killed himself) saw Jesus only in Galilee, on the mountain where he had told them to go.

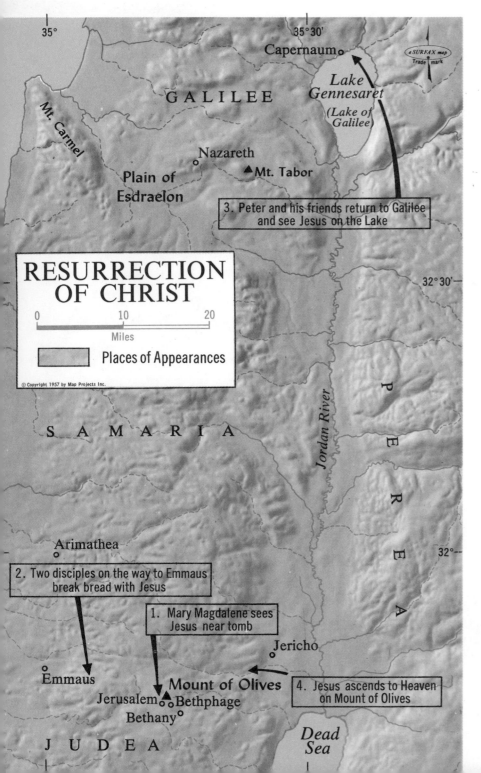

RESURRECTION OF CHRIST

0   10   20
Miles

☐ Places of Appearances

© Copyright 1957 by Map Projects Inc.

Capernaum

Lake Gennesaret (Lake of Galilee)

GALILEE

Mt. Carmel

Nazareth

Mt. Tabor

Plain of Esdraelon

3. Peter and his friends return to Galilee and see Jesus on the Lake

Jordan River

SAMARIA

P E R E A

Arimathea

2. Two disciples on the way to Emmaus break bread with Jesus

1. Mary Magdalene sees Jesus near tomb

Jericho

Emmaus

Mount of Olives

Jerusalem Bethphage

Bethany

4. Jesus ascends to Heaven on Mount of Olives

JUDEA

Dead Sea

THE RISEN CHRIST

In the gospel of Luke, however, Jesus appeared in Judea only. On the evening of the first day, two followers of Jesus, Cleopas and a friend, were walking to the village of Emmaus, northwest of Jerusalem. Jesus joined them on the way, as a stranger. They did not recognize him until he ate with them. Hurrying back to Jerusalem, the two men learned that Jesus had also shown himself to Simon Peter; and all of the followers of Jesus saw him that very night. It was apparently the next morning, when they were going to Bethany, that they saw him for the last time.

In the gospel of John, Jesus appeared on Sunday evening to the ten disciples—Thomas was not there—and eight days later to them all. John also tells the story of how Jesus revealed himself to some of the disciples along Lake Gennesaret.

THE CHURCH IN JERUSALEM

Seven weeks after the Passover, the followers of Jesus were gathered in Jerusalem for the feast of Pentecost (May–June, A.D. 29). There were about one hundred and twenty people, both men and women, and the *Acts of the Apostles* tells how suddenly the Holy Spirit took posses-

A typical garden tomb

sion of them. They must have assembled in a public place—probably a court of the temple—because a large number of Jews of the Dispersion, who were visiting Jerusalem for the festival, gathered around to watch and to listen. Some were astonished and puzzled by the disciples' behavior. Others mocked, thinking the disciples had drunk too much wine.

Peter, who had in a cowardly way denied knowing Jesus the night of his arrest, now courageously addressed the crowd. For the first time, the good news of Jesus Christ was preached publicly, and three thousand persons joined the disciples. It was the birthday of the church.

THE BEGINNINGS OF PERSECUTION

The first leaders and members of the church were still devoted Jews. Soon, however, difficulties arose between them and the officials of the temple. One afternoon, at the gate called "Beautiful," Peter and John healed in the name of Jesus a crippled beggar who had lain there for many years asking alms. The man followed them into the temple, leaping and praising God, and Peter started to preach to the crowd who gathered around. The captain of the temple police promptly had Peter and John arrested and thrown into jail.

A profile and plan of a garden tomb. Built into the side of a hill, it was approached by stairs (A), which led to the small, low opening of the tomb. The opening, usually covered by a stone, led to a small anteroom (B). In the last room (C) the body was put in a niche (D).

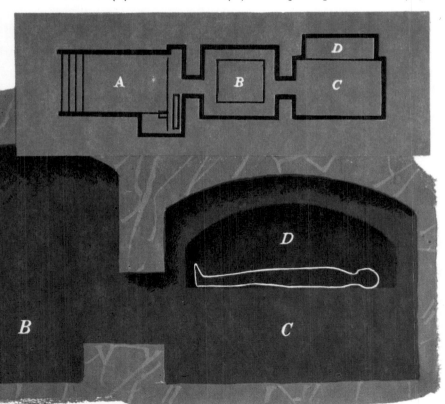

At his trial the next day, Peter spoke out boldly before the high priest and the Scribes. The authorities were afraid of the crowd, who were on Peter's side, and so they let the two men go with a stern warning. But Peter and the other disciples refused to be silent. They continued to preach and to heal the sick, and their fame spread to other towns of Judea outside Jerusa-

lem. When Peter was arrested a second time, he said to the high priest, "We must obey God rather than men." Without knowing it, he was separating himself from Judaism.

As the number of church members increased, the disciples had to appoint helpers, or deacons. Seven deacons were chosen from among the Greek-speaking Jews who had accepted the gospel; one of these was a man named Stephen.

Stephen was a fearless preacher. His preaching angered some of the strictly religious Jews, and he was stoned to death. Stephen was the first Christian martyr; his death marked the breaking point between Judaism and the new faith.

THE CHURCH IN JUDEA AND SAMARIA

Stephen's death was the signal for violent persecutions. These, however, only made the gospel spread. The disciples had to flee from Jerusalem, and they carried their new faith with them.

Philip, a deacon like Stephen, went to the city of Samaria. He healed and converted many who dwelt there. Then, journeying south on the road from Jerusalem to Gaza, Philip met a certain official of the Queen of Ethiopia, who was returning home in his chariot. This man seems to have been a Jewish convert; he was reading the *Book of Isaiah* as he rode. When Philip preached to him of Jesus, the Ethiopian believed and was baptized.

Philip preached the gospel throughout the Plain of Sharon, along the coast of the Mediterranean Sea, from Azotus (Ashdod) in the south to Caesarea in the north. Caesarea was a garrison town for the Roman soldiers, and the residence of the Roman procurators of Judea.

Some time later, Peter visited the new churches in that region, especially the church of Lydda. In Joppa he received word from a Roman captain named Cornelius to come to Caesarea. Peter went, and there he began to understand that God could accept a pagan as well as a Jew. The baptism of Cornelius marks the first time that a non-Jew was accepted as a follower of Jesus.

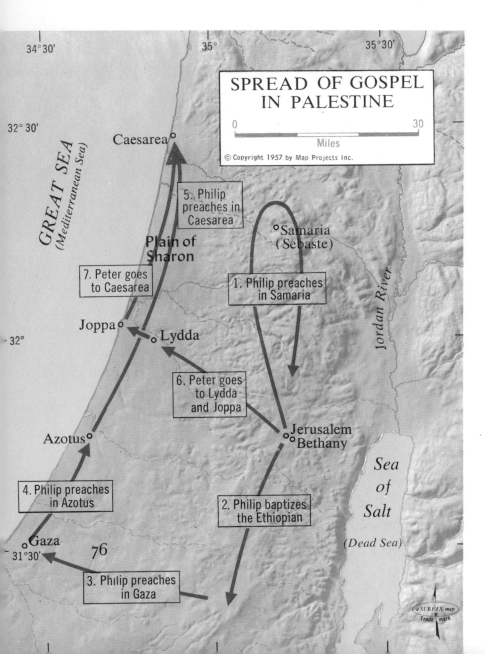

SPREAD OF GOSPEL IN PALESTINE

0   30

Miles

© Copyright 1957 by Map Projects Inc.

GREAT SEA (Mediterranean Sea)

Caesarea

5. Philip preaches in Caesarea

Samaria (Sebaste)

Plain of Sharon

7. Peter goes to Caesarea

1. Philip preaches in Samaria

Joppa

Lydda

Jordan River

6. Peter goes to Lydda and Joppa

Jerusalem
Bethany

Sea of Salt

(Dead Sea)

Azotus

4. Philip preaches in Azotus

2. Philip baptizes the Ethiopian

Gaza

76

3. Philip preaches in Gaza

Pompeian frieze

THE CONVERSION OF PAUL AND THE EARLY JOURNEYS

A.D. 35–51

Greek vase

Acts 9, 11-18, I and II Thessalonians

THE DEATH of Stephen and the persecution which followed did more than spread the gospel to Palestine. It spread the new faith to Damascus, Phoenicia, the island of Cyprus, and above all to Antioch, the metropolis of the north. In Antioch the followers of Jesus were first mockingly called "Christians."

THE CONVERSION OF SAUL, ABOUT A.D. 35

The death of Stephen probably had another effect, too. Among those who watched the mob murder him was a young Jew from Tarsus, named Saul (later to be known as Paul).

Tarsus, the capital of Cilicia in Asia Minor, was a center of trade and of Greek culture. Saul, a Roman citizen, had been educated at a Greek university, and was now in Jerusalem studying the religion of his fathers. As a Pharisee, he had no sympathy for Stephen, and at once threw himself into persecuting the Christians with great zeal and energy.

Not content with persecuting Christians in Jerusalem, he set out for Damascus to persecute them there. However, the memory of Stephen must have troubled Saul, for on the way to Damascus he had a vision of Christ in a blinding light. When he recovered, he was baptized as a Christian, and soon started preaching in the synagogues of Damascus that Jesus was the son of God. The Jews plotted to kill him, but his friends helped him escape, lowering him from the city wall at night in a basket.

Saul next went to Jerusalem, where he met Peter and also Barnabas, a Christian leader from Cyprus. But Jerusalem was too dangerous for Saul, and his friends took him to Caesarea, where he sailed for Tarsus. Barnabas went to Antioch, and found so much work to do that he sent for Saul to help him.

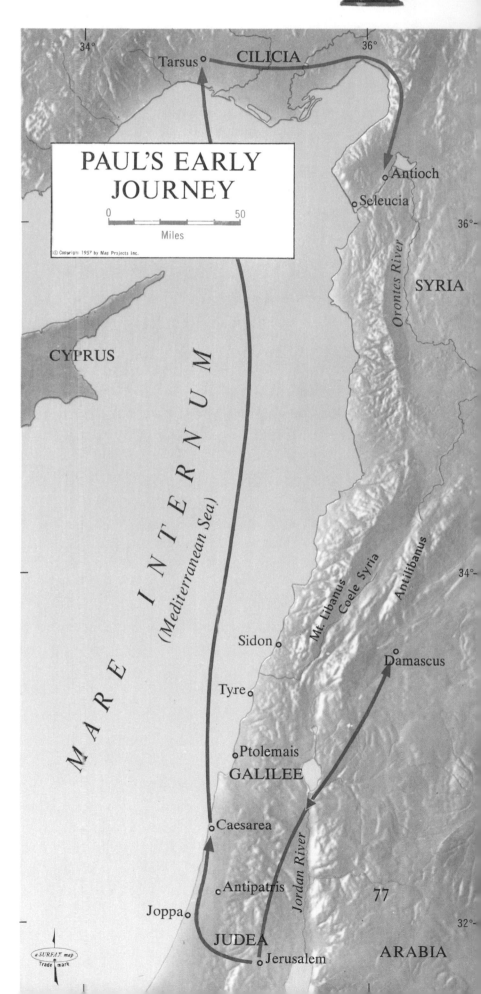

PAUL'S EARLY JOURNEY

0   50

Miles

© Copyright 1957 by Map Projects Inc.

Tarsus   CILICIA

Antioch

Seleucia

SYRIA

Orontes River

CYPRUS

MARE INTERNUM
(Mediterranean Sea)

Mt. Libanus   *Coele Syria*   *Antilibanus*

Sidon

Damascus

Tyre

Ptolemais

GALILEE

Jordan River

Caesarea

Antipatris

Joppa

JUDEA

Jerusalem

ARABIA

77

a SURFAX map
Trade mark

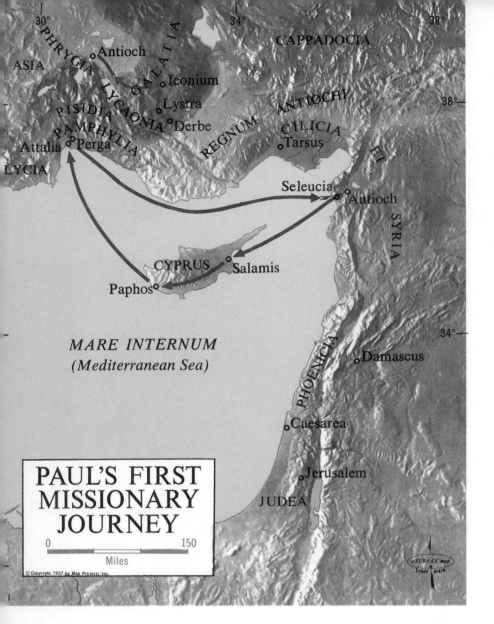

PAUL'S FIRST MISSIONARY JOURNEY

0   150

Miles

© Copyright 1957 by Map Projects Inc.

In the meantime, the church in Jerusalem was again in trouble. The young emperor Caligula of Rome had given Galilee and Perea to his friend Agrippa. A few years later, the emperor Claudius gave Agrippa the province of Judea also, and the title of king. Agrippa was a grandson of the Herod under whom Jesus had been born. He was eager to win the favor of the Jews. To do so, he persecuted the Christians. James, the brother of John, was beheaded; Peter was arrested, but escaped from jail. Fortunately for the benefit of the church, Agrippa soon fell ill and died (A.D. 44).

THE FIRST MISSIONARY JOURNEY—A.D. 45–46

During this time, Saul and Barnabas had been making many converts in Antioch. After a year, the church was so well established there that the two leaders decided to spread the faith elsewhere. They sailed for Cyprus, landed at Salamis, and went to Paphos. There they met the Roman proconsul, Sergius Paulus, "a man of

intelligence," who became a Christian. About this time, Saul changed his own name to Paul, perhaps in honor of the proconsul.

From Cyprus, Paul and Barnabas sailed to Asia Minor. They visited Perga, another city named Antioch in Pisidia, and Iconium. In all these cities, they went first to the synagogues to preach the new faith to the Jews. When the Jews cast them out, they made converts among the gentiles.

At Lystra, Paul healed a cripple, and the Greeks hailed him and Barnabas as gods. They believed that Barnabas was Zeus and that Paul, as his spokesman, was Hermes. The Jews, however, drove the missionaries out of Lystra, and they went on to Derbe.

From Derbe, Paul and Barnabas retraced their steps. At Attalia they took a ship for Antioch, where they reported to the church how God "had opened a door of faith to the gentiles."

One of the most serious questions in the early church was whether a gentile—that is, a pagan—could become a Christian without also becoming a Jew and being circumcised according to the Law of Moses. To settle this question, Barnabas, Paul, and Paul's young disciple Titus, an uncircumcised Greek, journeyed from Antioch to Jerusalem. There they met with the "pillars" of the church, and after long discussion it was agreed that gentiles who became Christians need not also become Jews. The Christian church was no longer part of Judaism. But many Jewish Christians were unhappy about this decision and found it hard to accept. Later, when Peter refused to eat with the uncircumcised, he was publicly rebuked by Paul.

THE SECOND MISSIONARY JOURNEY—A.D. 48–51

Returning to Antioch, Paul and Barnabas prepared to set out on another journey. They disagreed on which one of their friends to take with them. The two men therefore separated. Barnabas sailed for Cyprus, and Paul traveled by land to visit the churches of Asia Minor which he and Barnabas had founded.

Silas went with Paul. At Lystra a third disciple, Timothy, joined them. When they reached the harbor of Troas, Paul decided to preach the gospel in Greece, and they sailed across the Aegean Sea to Macedonia. With this voyage, Christianity spread from Asia to Europe.

At Philippi, the first large city where they preached, Paul and his companions were beaten and put in jail, but were released when the authorities learned that they were Roman citizens. At the next city, Thessalonica, the old story was repeated. They preached in the synagogues, but were driven out of town by some of the Jews, who were shocked by their message. The Jews at Beroea were more hospitable, and Silas and Timothy were able to remain there while Paul went on to Athens.

It was on the Areopagus—the Hill of Mars, opposite the Acropolis—that Paul made his famous speech to the Athenians on "the unknown God." But he was not very successful in Athens and soon left for Corinth, where he stayed a year and a half. At Corinth, he preached every Sabbath and worked at his trade of tentmaker. While living in that large city, he also wrote to

The word "acropolis" means "high city." On the Acropolis in Athens there were many beautiful buildings. The ruins still stand.

the Thessalonians twice (A.D. 50–51), telling them to work instead of waiting idly for the end of the world.

From Corinth, Paul sailed to Ephesus on the coast of Asia Minor, where he stayed only briefly but promised to come back. From Ephesus, he sailed to Caesarea, reported to the apostles in Jerusalem, and returned to Antioch.

PAUL'S SECOND MISSIONARY JOURNEY

0   300

Miles

© Copyright 1957 by Map Projects Inc.

MACEDONIA

THRACIA

(Black Sea)

Philippi · Neapolis
Thessalonica · Amphipolis
Beroea · Apollonia

Byzantium

BITHYNIA ET PONTUS

REGNUM POLEMONIS

MYSIA
Dorylaeum   GALATIA

ACHAIA (GREECE)

Mare Aegaeum
(Aegean Sea)

Troas

ASIA

CAPPADOCIA

PHRYGIA

Athens

Antioch

Cilician Gates

ANTIOCHI

Corinth
Cenchreae

Ephesus

Iconium
Lystra

Samos

PISIDIA
PAMPHYLIA

LYCAONIA
Derbe

REGNUM

CILICIA

Tarsus

Cnidus

LYCIA

Seleucia · Antioch

ET SYRIA

MARE INTERNUM
(Mediterranean Sea)

CRETE

Salamis
CYPRUS

Paphos

Sidon   Damascus

Caesarea

Antipatris

25°   30°   35°

Temple of Artemis at Ephesus

PAUL'S LATER JOURNEYS

A.D. 52–62

*Acts 19–29, Galatians, I and II Corinthians,
Romans, Philippians, Colossians, Philemon*

FOR A WHILE, Paul remained in Antioch. Then he decided to visit once again the Christian communities he had founded.

THE THIRD JOURNEY—EPHESUS AND GREECE

Passing through Galatia and Phrygia (A.D. 52) Paul went to Ephesus, keeping his earlier promise.

Paul stayed at Ephesus for three years, A.D. 53–56. In Ephesus stood one of the seven wonders of the ancient world, the splendid temple of the goddess Artemis, or Diana, where many visitors came to worship.

As usual, Paul started by preaching in the synagogues. Then he moved to a meeting place where he could speak to both Jews and Gentiles. Christian groups were established not only in Ephesus but in many nearby places.

The years at Ephesus seem to have been years of great suffering for Paul, in both mind and body. To add to his other troubles, enemies were at work against him in the churches of Galatia and Corinth. He wrote a letter to the Galatians, urging them to be tolerant. In A.D. 54 he wrote the Corinthians a letter of advice, now lost. The following spring he wrote them a second letter (*I Corinthians*).

Paul's work in Ephesus was ended by a riot. The silversmiths of the city feared that his preaching against idols would take away their

80

business of making shrines for Artemis. They stirred up a mob that chanted for two hours, "Great is the Artemis of the Ephesians!" Finally a city official quieted the people and sent them away without harm.

After the riot, public opinion in Ephesus was no longer favorable. In the summer or autumn of A.D. 56, Paul set out for Greece.

He spent the winter in Corinth, trying vainly to settle the quarrels in that church. Facing a deadlock, he went on to Macedonia, and from there wrote the Corinthians a harsh letter (now *II Corinthians* 10–16) and, soon afterwards a friendly letter (now *II Corinthians* 1–9).

Paul began to dream of going to Rome, and sent the Christians there a letter which is one of the best explanations of Christian faith ever written. But first, he wanted to go back to Jerusalem. He sailed for home in the spring of A.D. 57, stopping at Miletus to say farewell to the elders of the church at Ephesus, whom he felt he would never see again.

Ruins of the Temple of Apollo at Corinth, Greece—part of the Roman colony of Achaia at the time Paul preached there.

The ship put in at Tyre to unload its cargo, and Paul made the rest of the journey by land, stopping at Ptolemais and Caesarea. Although friends at Caesarea warned him that attempts would be made against his life, Paul deliberately went up to Jerusalem.

PAUL'S THIRD MISSIONARY JOURNEY

0   300

Miles

© Copyright 1957 by Map Projects Inc.

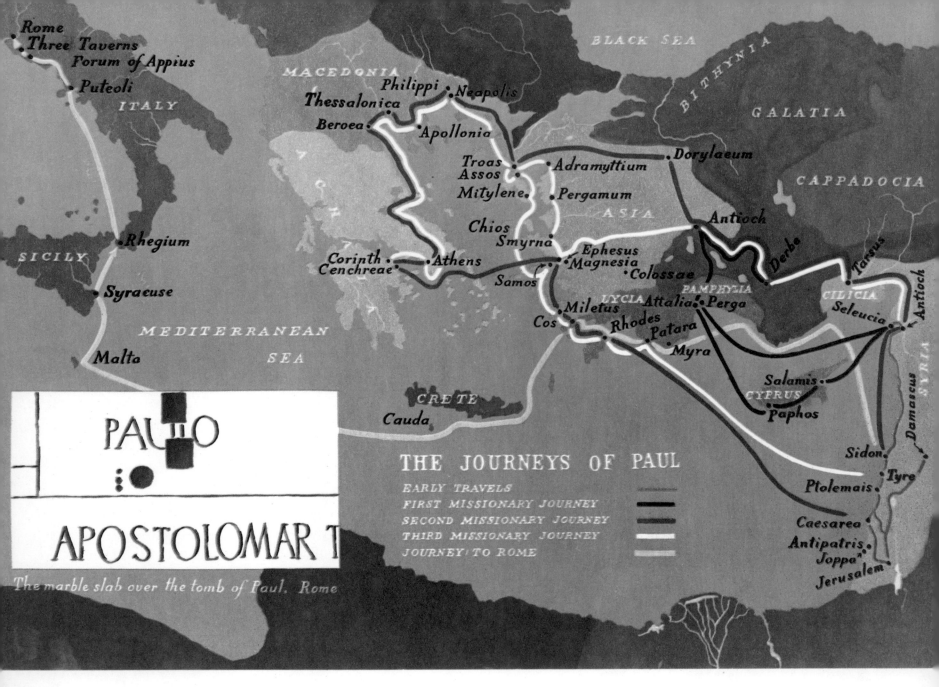

THE JOURNEYS OF PAUL

EARLY TRAVELS
FIRST MISSIONARY JOURNEY
SECOND MISSIONARY JOURNEY
THIRD MISSIONARY JOURNEY
JOURNEY TO ROME

The marble slab over the tomb of Paul, Rome

THE ARREST IN THE TEMPLE, A.D. 57

It was the feast of Pentecost, an important religious season when Jews from far lands were returning to the holy land. Among these homecomers were some Jews from Ephesus. These men had seen Paul on the streets in the company of Trophimus, an uncircumcised Greek from Ephesus. When they found Paul in the inner court of the temple, they were sure that he had brought Trophimus in with him. According to Jewish law, such an act was an extremely grave one—punishable by death.

At the outcry raised by the Ephesians, the mob dragged Paul out of the temple to kill him. The Roman tribune Claudius Lysias heard the commotion and rescued Paul, allowing him to address the crowd. The people would not listen, however, and the puzzled official could only lock Paul up in the Antonia Fortress overnight.

The next day, the tribune set Paul before the Jewish chief priests and the council. An uproar broke out. The tribune, learning of a new plot on Paul's life, sent him under guard to Antonius Felix, the Roman governor, at Caesarea.

Felix knew something about the Christian faith and seemed friendly to Paul, but he did not wish to offend the Jews by letting Paul go. As a result, two years later, when Felix was succeeded by a new Roman governor, Porcius Festus, Paul was still a prisoner.

Festus offered to send Paul to Jerusalem to stand trial. As a Roman citizen, Paul claimed the right to be tried by the emperor in Rome. At this point, King Agrippa II of Chalcis and his sister Bernice came to visit Festus, who was trying to decide what to write to the emperor about Paul. Festus therefore had Paul appear before his royal visitors. Paul spoke so brilliantly that, in spite of himself, Agrippa was deeply impressed. Both he and Festus agreed that if only Paul had not appealed to Rome for a trial, he could have been released.

THE JOURNEY TO ROME, A.D. 59–60

With other prisoners, Paul was put in the custody of a centurion named Julius. The party set sail on a ship bound for Adramyttium, a port in Asia Minor. After touching at Sidon, they passed near Cyprus and landed at Myra. There they boarded a ship going from Alexandria to Italy.

At first, for lack of wind, navigation was slow. They followed the coast as far as Cnidus, and then turned southward and stopped at Fair Havens in Crete. The harbor was not well sheltered and the stormy winter season had begun. The captain of the ship sailed for Phoenix, hoping to spend the winter there. Then a terrific gale, called the "northeaster," struck. For thirteen days, the little ship was driven by wind and waves far off its course. On the fourteenth day, however, it ran aground off a beach. Reaching shore, the passengers and crew learned that they were on the island of Malta.

Three months later they boarded another ship, the *Castor and Pollux*. They touched Sicily at Syracuse and the foot of Italy at Rhegium. From Rhegium, a good south wind sent them straight to Puteoli, in the Bay of Naples.

News of Paul's coming had already reached the Christians in Rome. As Paul and his party neared the city, some of the Christians came out along the Appian Way to meet them, as far as the Forum of Appius and Three Taverns.

Paul reached Rome in February, A.D. 60. Waiting for his trial before the Emperor Nero, he lived there for at least two years, in a house which he had rented. It was probably from Rome that he wrote a letter to the Philippians in Macedonia, another to the Colossians in Phrygia, and a short note to his friend Philemon. Although guarded by a soldier, he was apparently almost free. In the world's capital he "welcomed all who came to him, preaching the kingdom of God and teaching about the Lord Jesus Christ quite openly and unhindered."

The Appian Way, the main road leading from Rome to Greece and the East, was more than 350 miles long. It was made of stone blocks which were cemented together.

THE CHURCH AT THE END OF THE FIRST CENTURY

A.D. 62–100

*I and II Timothy, Titus, Hebrews, James,
I Peter, I—III John, Jude, Revelation*

Decorations from the catacombs

THE *Acts of the Apostles* ends with Paul preaching and teaching in Rome. According to one tradition, Paul was beheaded in Rome in A.D. 64, when the Emperor Nero was persecuting the Christians, and Peter was crucified there at the same time.

It is also possible that Paul was freed, and made at least two more missionary journeys. One of these may have been westward to Spain, and the other eastward to Ephesus, Macedonia, and the island of Crete. Some of Paul's short notes to Timothy and Titus, his disciples, may have been written in A.D. 60–75. They were later preserved in the longer epistles to Timothy and Titus—the so-called Pastoral Epistles.

THE DESTRUCTION OF JERUSALEM

While Paul was vigorously carrying the gospel to the gentiles, trouble was brewing in Jerusalem. The Jewish aristocracy (the Sadducees and the high priests), the scholars (the Scribes), and the Pharisees had finally accepted the Roman rule. But the Zealots could not be won over. In A.D. 66 there was a general revolt.

The Roman general Vespasian, and later his son Titus, put down the revolt with all the harshness of the Roman army. In A.D. 70, Jerusalem was captured and the temple was burned to the ground. Judaism survived in synagogues, but it no longer had its center in one holy place. The Dispersion was at last complete.

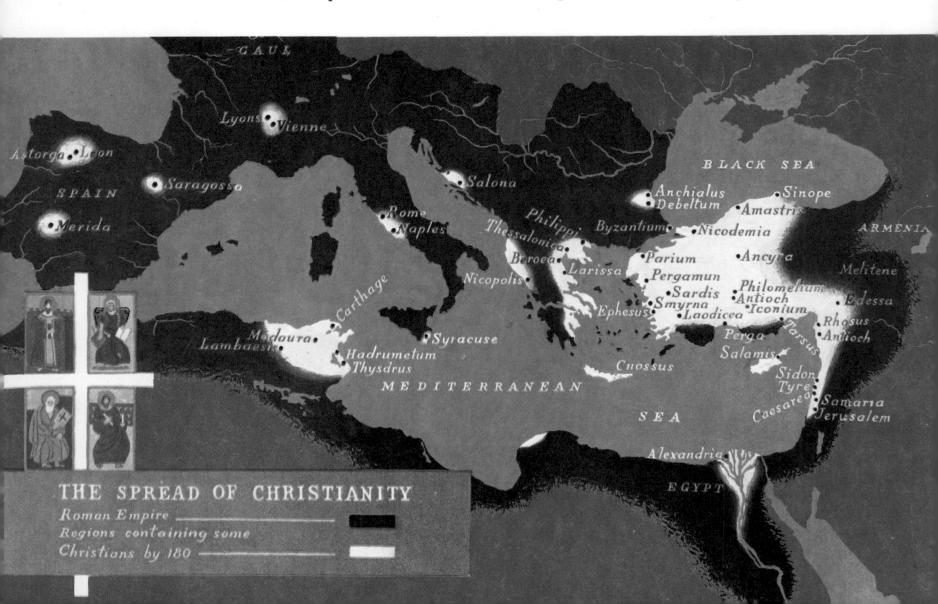

THE SPREAD OF CHRISTIANITY

Roman Empire

Regions containing some
Christians by 180

THE GROWTH OF THE CHURCH, A.D. 70–100

The Jewish Christian community had left Jerusalem at the beginning of the revolt in A.D. 66, going to Pella in Transjordan. To the Christians as well as to the Jews, the destruction of the temple was important. It marked the final break between Judaism and Christianity.

There is practically no information on the spread of the gospel around the Mediterranean Sea in the second half of the first century. Alexandria and Antioch were the great Christian centers in the east; and Ephesus, Corinth, and Rome in the west. According to *I Peter*, Christian communities flourished even in Bithynia, Cappadocia, and Pontus. By the end of the first century A.D., the gospel had been preached in North Africa, in Spain, and in Gaul.

No formal "church government" bound these scattered communities together. Yet the Christians felt united. They thought of themselves as the "remnant" announced by the prophet Isaiah of old. Like the Hebrews at the time of Moses, these men and women felt that they were "a chosen people, a holy nation." Their mission was "to proclaim the power of one who had called them from darkness into his marvelous light."

THE BOOK OF REVELATION

Under the Roman emperors, such a mission took courage. Anyone becoming a Christian risked torture and death. Knowing this, John the Divine wrote from the island of Patmos to seven churches in Asia Minor. A prisoner himself, he comforted them with his prophesy of the fall of "Babylon" (Rome), and his vision of the New Jerusalem, where God would dwell with men and death would be no more.

The Tree of Life in the Garden of Eden, from which man was expelled, becomes the "tree" of Golgotha, and again the tree of life whose "leaves are for the healing of nations."

THE TWO TESTAMENTS

The books of the New Testament probably date from A.D. 50 to 150. Gradually the Christians of the first century began to gather together some writings which they read at their assem-

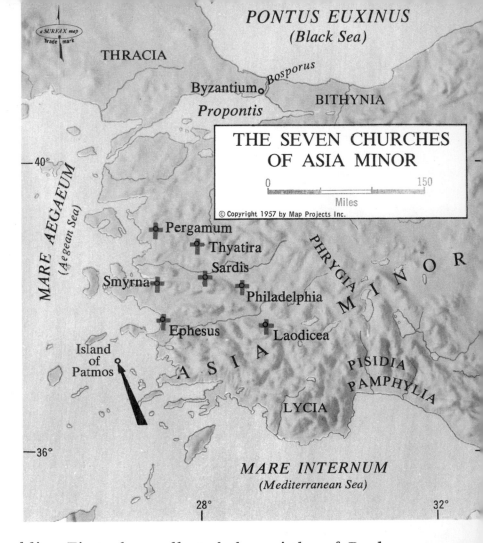

blies. First, they collected the epistles of Paul. They then wrote down all that could be remembered about the life and sayings of Jesus, and the early church in Jerusalem. These were the gospels and the *Acts of the Apostles*. A few other writings were also included, and the whole was added to the Septuagint, the Greek translation of the Hebrew Old Testament.

The Old Testament is much older than the New. The first five books, the Pentateuch, were probably written down between 1000 B.C. and 397 B.C. In Judaism these five books are called "The Law."

The second major section of the Old Testament, "The Prophets," may have been in written form by 220 B.C. This group of books includes *Joshua, Judges, Samuel,* and *Kings,* as well as the prophetic writings. At the time of Jesus, the Jewish holy books included only the Law and the Prophets.

However, at the end of the first century A.D., Jewish scholars added *Psalms, Proverbs, Job, The Song of Songs, Ruth, Lamentations, Ecclesiastes, Esther, Daniel, Ezra, Nehemiah,* and *Chronicles* to their holy writings. These books also found their way into the Christian Bible.

85

DIGGING INTO THE PAST

CITIES OF THE BIBLE REDISCOVERED

UNTIL MODERN TIMES, almost nothing was known about the lands and peoples of the Bible except what the Bible itself told. Many of the ancient cities had disappeared.

The first step toward rediscovering this lost world was taken by Napoleon Bonaparte. In his Egyptian campaign of 1798, he included, along with his soldiers, a large party of scientists, artists, and scholars to study the temples and monuments of the Nile Valley. This expedition found the famous "Rosetta Stone," from which, in 1822, the Frenchman Champollion finally learned how to read Egyptian hieroglyphics.

By 1857, three other men had solved the mystery of the cuneiform ("wedge-shaped") writing of the ancient inhabitants of Mesopotamia. Scholars could now read many inscriptions and documents of Egypt and Mesopotamia that shed light on Biblical times.

Much has also been learned about the vanished Bible cities of Palestine from archaeological excavation. Before they could be dug up, however, these places had to be found. Sometimes the sites could be recognized from the names of the modern Arab villages built near by.

An American, Edward Robinson of Union Theological Seminary in New York, was the pioneer in the modern science of Biblical geography. Traveling on horseback and on foot, in 1838 and 1852 he located hundreds of Biblical places. His work has been carried on by American, British, French, and German scholars. In the past twenty years, Nelson Glueck of the Hebrew Union College in Cincinnati has found many additional sites in the Jordan valley, Transjordan, and the Negeb.

Some of the towns had been destroyed and rebuilt several times. The rebuilders did not clear away the ashes, dirt, and ruins of the old town; they merely built the new one on top. The result was a mound, sometimes ninety feet high.

In digging at such a place, archaeologists can clear the mound off layer by layer. Or, more often, they cut trenches at carefully selected spots, and thus get a cross section of the different towns built on the site.

Usually, the top ruins are those of the Turkish or Arab town, built from the thirteenth century A.D. to the present. Below these are ruins dating from the time of the Crusades (eleventh to thirteenth centuries); and below them are the ruins of the city during the Byzantine period (fourth to eighth centuries). Then, farther down, and therefore farther back in time, are uncovered in turn the traces of the Roman, Maccabean, Hellenistic, Persian, Neo-Babylonian, Israelite, and finally Canaanite occupations.

In a few cities, deep levels are reached which tell of peoples older than the Canaanites. At Jericho, probably the oldest city in Palestine, there are even traces of prehistoric man. At last, on any site, the diggers reach virgin soil or bed rock. Then they know that they have come to the beginning of human occupancy in that particular spot.

These are some of the art objects that lay buried under the soil of the Holy Land until archeologists dug them up and identified them. From objects like these, we can learn much about the culture of its early inhabitants.

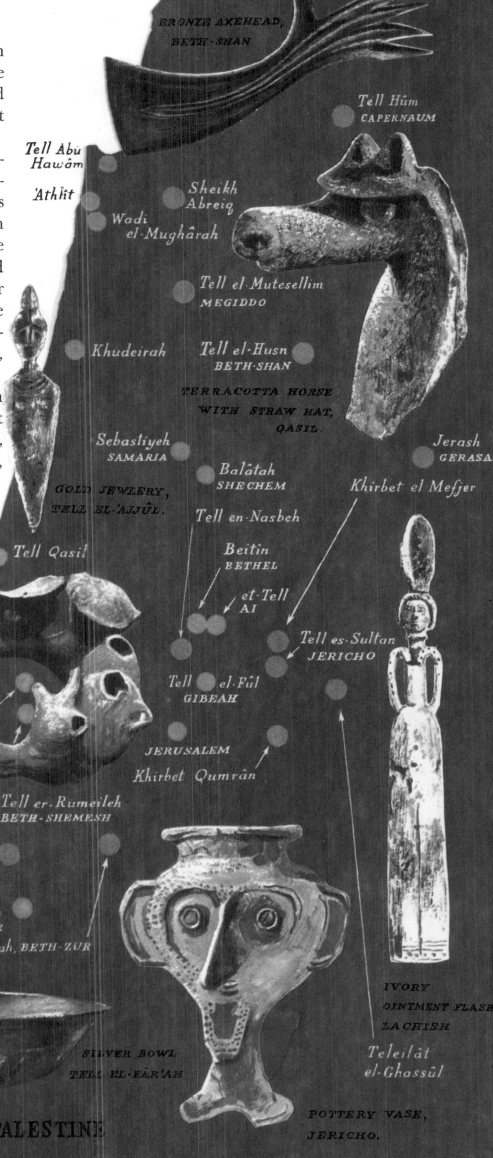

BRONZE AXEHEAD, BETH-SHAN

Tell Hûm
CAPERNAUM

Tell Abu Hawâm

'Athlit

Sheikh Abreiq

Wadi el-Mughârah

Tell el-Mutesellim
MEGIDDO

Khudeirah

Tell el-Husn
BETH-SHAN

TERRACOTTA HORSE WITH STRAW HAT, QASIL.

Jerash
GERASA

Sebastiyeh
SAMARIA

Balâtah
SHECHEM

Khirbet el Mefjer

GOLD JEWLERY, TELL EL-'AJJÛL.

Tell en-Nasbeh

Tell Qasil

Beitin
BETHEL

et-Tell
AI

Tell es-Sultan
JERICHO

Tell el-Fûl
GIBEAH

KERNOS RING MEGIDDO.

JERUSALEM

Khirbet Qumrân

Tell Jezer
GEZER

Tell er-Rumeileh
BETH-SHEMESH

Asqalan
ASHKELON

Tell ed-Duweir
LACHISH

Tell Beit Mirsim
DEBIR

Khirbet et Tubeiqah, BETH-ZUR

SEAL IMPRESSION, DEBIR

GAZA
Tell el-'Ajjul
Tell Jemmeh

Tell el-Fâr'ah
SHARUHEN

IVORY OINTMENT FLASK LACHISH

Teleilât el-Ghassûl

SILVER BOWL TELL EL-FÂR'AH

POTTERY VASE, JERICHO.

ARCHEOLOGICAL EXCAVATIONS IN PALESTINE

Early Bronze

Middle Bronze

Late Bronze

Iron Age I

Iron Age II

In each layer of a buried city, many things are found. There are bits of broken pots, statues, jewelry, and objects of everyday life. From these, the archaeologists can tell a great deal about the people who lived there.

The bits of pottery are especially important. The shape of the handle and neck of a pitcher, the kind of clay used, the way the piece was fired, and the painting or finish on the surface—these details are different for each period. Scientists are able to tell with great accuracy when a broken piece of pottery was made. In this way they date the layer in which it was found.

Specialists have learned, for example, that the city of Megiddo (the modern Tell el-Mutesellim) has been taken, destroyed and rebuilt nineteen times since 3500 B.C. Twenty layers of ruins were found there, between layers of ashes and debris. Megiddo was on a pass between the coastal plain of Sharon and the valley of Esdraelon (Jezreel) southwest of Mount Carmel. It occupied one of the key points in the Fertile Crescent, and was a prize often fought for. It is therefore easy to understand why the name "Har-megiddo" (Hill of Megiddo) became the Bible's name for the last bloody battle of history—"Armageddon."

Another way to date ruins is by the stones of walls and buildings. The stonecutters and masons of different periods used different tools and methods of cutting. Thus a corner of a building that can be identified as Saul's fortress was unearthed at his old stronghold of Gibeah (Tell el-Fûl). In the oldest part of Jerusalem, portions of the ancient walls have been brought to light. Some belong to the Jebusite castle of the Canaanite period; some are David's and Solomon's repairs and additions. Part of Nehemiah's wall has been found; and still other walls were those built by the King Herod in whose reign Jesus was born. From such ancient walls and buildings, drawings or models have been made showing how several ancient cities of Palestine must have looked.

Examples of pottery from the Early Bronze through the Iron Age.

INSCRIPTIONS IN PALESTINE

Inscriptions also have been found which tell of life in Bible times. For example, a calendar written a few years after the death of Solomon was found at Gezer (Tell Jezer). It was a kind of farmer's almanac, giving the proper times to take care of olive trees, barley, flax, fruits, and vineyards. The Moabite Stone, the monument of Mesha, King of Moab, tells about his troubles with Israel around 850 B.C.

There is a fascinating so-called "Siloam Inscription" on the wall of the tunnel which King Hezekiah (about 715-687 B.C.) had dug to bring the waters of Gihon to the pool of Siloam inside Jerusalem. The inscription tells how two parties of workmen, starting from opposite sides of the hill, dug through the rock and met underground, each party guided by the sound of the other's pickaxes.

Letters written on broken pieces of pottery were found at Lachish (Tell ed-Duweir). These letters had probably been sent to the military commander of Lachish from Jerusalem, then under Babylonian siege, just before Jerusalem fell in 586 B.C.

MANUSCRIPTS OF OLD TESTAMENT BOOKS

Until recent years, the manuscripts from which the Old Testament text of the modern Bibles was translated were all late copies. The earliest known Hebrew texts of the Old Testament were Jewish scrolls of the Middle Ages, none going back before the tenth century A.D.

In modern times, however, fragments of earlier manuscripts have been found, especially in Cairo, Egypt. From 1947 to the present, there have been exciting finds in the caves of the Wadi Qumrân near the Dead Sea. Among other scrolls, there were Hebrew copies of the *Book of Isaiah,* which may date from the first century B.C. In addition, thousands of fragments from other Old Testament books were discovered, which are now being studied by Biblical scholars.

Biblical archaeology has thus already brought a rich harvest. In the years to come, it may be expected to tell even more about the ancient Hebrews and the early Christians.

Dead Sea Scrolls

Gezer Calendar

Moabite Stone

Lachish Letters

"Siloam Inscription"

The Dome of the Rock

THE HOLY LAND OF THREE FAITHS

THE COUNTRY of the Bible is today a "holy land" for three faiths: Judaism, Christianity, and Islam. All have shrines there.

The Jewish monuments are the fewest in number. Like the temple, most of them were destroyed by warfare. After the fall of Jerusalem in A.D. 70 and the repression of the final uprising under the Jewish leader Bar-Cochba in A.D. 135, most of the Jews who remained in Palestine lived in Galilee. For several centuries they maintained a center of learning in Tiberias. The synagogue in Capernaum dates from about the third century A.D. In Jerusalem, part of the foundation wall for the temple enclosure has been uncovered. Known as the "Wailing Wall," it was probably built in Herod's time.

EARLY CHRISTIAN SHRINES

After the emperor Constantine recognized Christianity as the official religion of his empire in A.D. 313, many men and women went to Palestine to live and die near the "holy places." Shrines were built in honor of Christ by Constantine himself, by his mother Helena, by the empress Eudocia in the fifth century A.D., and by the emperor Justinian, who died in A.D. 565.

This period is called the Byzantine Age, from Byzantium (Constantinople), where these emperors maintained their capital. Helena's Basilica (church) of the Nativity in Bethlehem is still standing, and ruins of other Byzantine churches have been discovered in Jerusalem, Bethany, Emmaus, Nazareth, and Cana. Most of them were burned down in the seventh century.

MOSLEM SHRINES

Since Islam, or Mohammedanism, shares many of the basic beliefs of Judaism and Christianity, Palestine is a "holy land" for Moslems also. One of the most important Moslem shrines is the Mosque of Omar in Jerusalem.

The rocky threshing-floor bought by David for the altar of the Lord has had a curious history. It was the site of the temple of Solomon and of the later temple. In A.D. 135, the emperor Hadrian built a shrine to Jupiter there. When the new religion of Mohammed spread through the Near East, the Caliph Omar selected this holy rock as the site for a mosque. Built in A.D. 691, the Dome of the Rock was damaged by an earthquake in 1027, but has been restored.

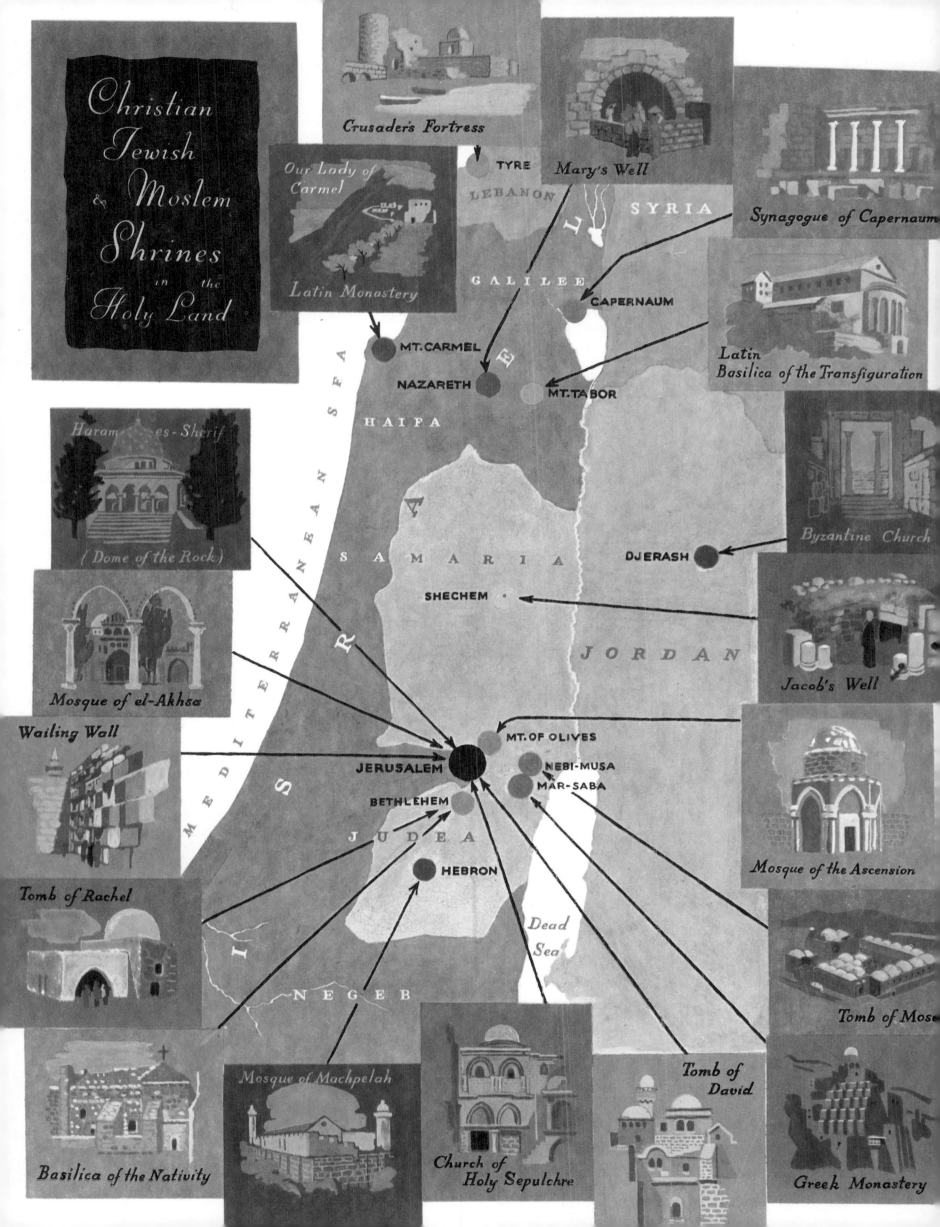

Christian
Jewish
& Moslem
Shrines
in the
Holy Land

Crusader's Fortress

Mary's Well

Synagogue of Capernaum

Our Lady of
Carmel

Latin Monastery

TYRE

LEBANON

SYRIA

GALILEE

CAPERNAUM

Latin
Basilica of the Transfiguration

MT. CARMEL

MEDITERRANEAN SEA

NAZARETH

MT. TABOR

HAIFA

Haram es-Sherif

(Dome of the Rock)

SAMARIA

DJERASH

Byzantine Church

SHECHEM

JORDAN

Jacob's Well

Mosque of el-Akhsa

ISRAEL

Wailing Wall

MT. OF OLIVES

JERUSALEM

NEBI-MUSA

MAR-SABA

BETHLEHEM

JUDEA

Mosque of the Ascension

Tomb of Rachel

HEBRON

Dead
Sea

NEGEB

Tomb of Moses

Basilica of the Nativity

Mosque of Machpelah

Church of
Holy Sepulchre

Tomb of
David

Greek Monastery

An Israeli reforestation program

Also sacred to Islam is the mosque at Hebron, which shelters the traditional graves of Abraham, Isaac, and Jacob. The so-called Tomb of Rachel and the Tomb of Samuel are handsome Arab structures of the Middle Ages.

LATER CHRISTIAN SHRINES

For nearly a century (1099 to 1187), the Crusaders held the Holy Land. They built the present Basilica of the Holy Sepulchre in Jerusalem. The Crusaders' church has had several awkward additions built onto it for the use of various Christian denominations.

Many other churches were erected in Palestine by Greek Orthodox and Roman monastic orders during the Middle Ages and in more recent years. Several are in and around Jerusalem. One of the best is the small pavilion, now a

A dam on the Jordan River

mosque, of the Crusaders' Church of the Ascension on the Mount of Olives.

THE HOLY LAND TODAY

The Kingdom of the Frankish Knights was overthrown in 1187, when the Saracens under Saladin defeated the Crusaders' army at Hattin near Tiberias. Since then, the Holy Land has been conquered by still other invaders, especially the Mongols (1268) and the Turks (1516). A Turkish sultan, Suleiman the Magnificent, built the present walls of Jerusalem in the sixteenth century.

From the seventh century A.D., when the Sassanid Persians overran the country, Palestine became a ruined land. Under the Turks, trees were taxed, and so the farmers cut them down. Rain washed the soil off the hillsides, and valleys once fertile became deserts. For centuries, Palestine looked very little like the "promised land" of the Bible.

However, after 1920 the British and the Zionists started a reclamation program which has been continued since 1948 by the State of Israel.

The soil is being improved by the use of fertilizers and good farming practices. Erosion of the soil is being controlled by terracing and irrigation. New forests have been planted and will soon produce timber.

The country is beginning to regain its ancient greenness and prosperity. Groves of citrus fruit flourish in the Jordan valley and on the plains of Jezreel and Sharon. The dry and torrid Negeb, south of the ancient town of Beer-sheba, is being irrigated and cleared of stones for planting. In just a few years' time, "the desert shall bloom like a rose."

Today, people of three faiths, scattered all over the world, still look upon the ancient land of Canaan as the Holy Land. Jews, Christians and Moslems might well remember the words of the Psalmist of old:

"Pray for the peace of Jerusalem!"

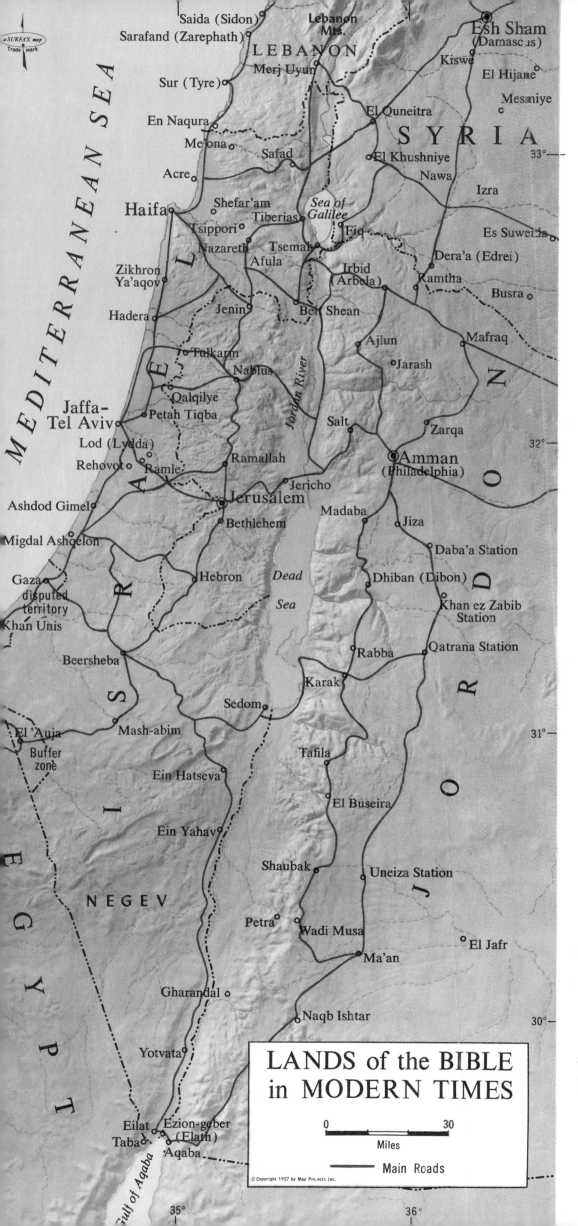

(The indicated boundaries of Israel are in dispute.)

The agriculture of Israel today is a diversified one. In addition to the citrus fruits, grapes, and olives that were formerly Palestine's chief products, Israel also raises grain (wheat and barley), vegetables, and bananas, and dairying and poultry raising are also important. Most of these products are raised on a cooperative basis on communal farms. Roads serve as the chief means of transportation, although a main railroad runs up the entire coast.

The outstanding geographic feature of Jordan is that it lies entirely along the Jordan valley, the deepest depression in the world. Much of the land is barren desert, and only a small percentage of it is under cultivation. It is hoped that with irrigation and reforestation much of its former fertility will be restored.

LANDS of the BIBLE
in MODERN TIMES

0   30
Miles
— Main Roads

© Copyright 1957 by Map Projects Inc.

Jewish Lamp

OLD TESTAMENT HISTORY

Paleolithic Age (Early Stone Age) About 200,000-25,000 B.C.

Mesolithic Age (Middle Stone Age) About 25,000-8000 B.C. Beginnings of agriculture.

Neolithic Age (Late Stone Age) About 8000-4500 B.C. General use of pottery.

Chalcolithic Age (Stone and Copper Age) About 4500-3000 B.C. Copper and stone tools.

	WEST	PALESTINE	EAST
3000 B.C.	EGYPT	CANAAN	MESOPOTAMIA
Early Bronze Age	Early Dynasties 3000-2700. Old Kingdom 2700-2200. THE GREAT PYRAMIDS First Intermediate Age 2200-2000. AMORITE (?) INVADERS FROM ASIA		First Sumerian Kings 2800-2400 First Semite Kings 2400-2000 *Sargon of Agade* Sumerian Revival 2200-2000 THE KINGS OF UR
2000 B.C.			
Middle Bronze Age	Middle Kingdom 2000-1780 Second Intermediate Age 1780-1550 HYKSOS INVADERS FROM ASIA	Egyptian Control of Canaan *Abraham, Isaac, Jacob, Joseph* *Oral Traditions of* *the Hebrew Fathers*	Amorite Kingdom of Babylon 2000-1700 *Hammurabi* HITTITE INVADERS FROM ASIA MINOR 1700-1550
1500 B.C.			
Late Bronze Age	New Kingdom 1546-1200 B.C. *Amenophis IV 1370-1353* *Seti I 1319-1301* *Ramses II 1301-1234* *Merneptah 1224-1216*	Tell el-Amarna Letters (*The Habiru*) HEBREW CONQUEST OF CANAAN 1235-1200 *Oral Traditions of the Exodus, the* *Wandering in the Wilderness, and the Conquest*	Kassite Rule of Southern Mesopotamia 1500-1150 Hurrian Rule of Northern Mesopotamia 1500-1370 Hittite Rule 1370-1250
1200 B.C.			
Early Iron Age		The Judges about 1235-1020 *The Song of Deborah about 1125* PHILISTINE INVADERS ABOUT 1100 *Samuel about 1050-1020* *Oral Traditions of the Judges and the Ark at Shechem and Shiloh* *Saul about 1020-1002* THE UNITED KINGDOM OF ISRAEL	Rise of Assyria in Northern Mesopotamia 1250-1000 *Tiglath-pileser I about 1100 B.C.*
1000 B.C.			
Beginning of written Old Testament Court memoirs, royal archives, temple records, writing down of oral tradition.		*David 1002-962* *Solomon 962-922* BUILDING OF THE TEMPLE SHISHAK'S INVASION 922-921 (?) THE DIVIDED KINGDOMS 922-722	Assyrian Empire 1000-612
		KINGDOM OF JUDAH	KINGDOM OF ISRAEL	
		Rehoboam 922-915 *Abijah 915-913*	*Jeroboam 922-901* *Nadab 901-900*	
900 B.C.			
Early Law Codes *Oral Traditions of Elijah and Elisha*	*Asa 913-873* *Jehoshaphat 873-849* *Jehoram 849-842* *Ahaziah 842* *Athaliah 842-837* *Joash 837-800*	*Baasha 900-877* *Elah 877* *Omri 877-869* *Ahab 869-850* *Ahaziah 850-849* *Joram 849-842* *Jehu 842-815* *Jehoahaz 815-801*	ASSYRIAN INVASION OF SYRIA 890 BATTLE OF QARQAR 853 *Shalmaneser III 859-824*
800 B.C.			

PALESTINE	EAST	
		800 B.C.

PALESTINE   EAST

CANAAN   MESOPOTAMIA

800 B.C.

KINGDOM OF JUDAH	KINGDOM OF ISRAEL	MESOPOTAMIA	
Amaziah 800-783	*Jehoash 801-786*		*Amos, Hosea*
Uzziah 783-742	*Jeroboam 786-746*	FALL OF DAMASCUS 732	*Isaiah: Early Oracles*
Jotham 742-735	*Zechariah 746-745*	*Tiglath-pileser III 845-727*	
Ahaz 735-715	*Menahem 745-738*	*Shalmaneser V 727-722*	
Hezekiah 715-687	*Pekahiah 738-737*	*Sargon II 722-705*	
	Pekah 737-732		
	Hoshea 732-722		

FALL OF SAMARIA AND THE END OF
THE KINGDOM OF ISRAEL 722

700 B.C.

Manasseh 687-642	*Sennacherib 705-681*	*Isaiah: Later Oracles*
Amon 642-640	*Esarhaddon 681-669*	*Micah, Deuteronomy*
Josiah 640-609	*Ashurbanipal 669-630*	*Zephaniah, Nahum*
Jehoiakim 609-597	FALL OF NINEVEH 612	*Habakkuk*
		Jeremiah, I-II Kings

600 B.C.

	BATTLE OF CARCHEMISH 605	
Zedekiah 597-586	*Nebuchadnezzar 604-562*	*Ezekiel*
FALL OF JERUSALEM 586	*Evil-merodach 562-560*	*Lamentations*
BABYLONIAN CAPTIVITY 586-539	*Nabonidus 556-539*	*Samuel*
Sheshbazzar, Zerubbabel	*Babylonian Empire 612-539*	*Isaiah 40-55*
	FALL OF BABYLON 539	*Job, Joshua*
TEMPLE REBUILT 521-516	Persian Empire	*Haggai*
	Cyrus 539-530	*Zechariah 1-8*
	Cambyses 530-522	*Isaiah 56-66*
	Darius I 522-486	

500 B.C.

EZRA'S FIRST VISIT TO JERUSALEM 458	*Xerxes I 486-465*	*Nehemiah*
NEHEMIAH'S REBUILDING OF	*Artaxerxes I 465-424*	*Joel*
THE WALLS OF JERUSALEM 445-443	*Darius II 423-404*	*Malachi*

400 B.C.

EZRA'S SECOND VISIT TO JERUSALEM 397	*Artaxerxes II 404-358*	*Pentateuch, Chronicles*
JERUSALEM TAKEN BY ALEXANDER 333	*Artaxerxes III 358-338*	*Ruth, Jonah*
	Defeat of Darius III 331	*Ezra, Psalms*

WEST

300 B.C.

GREECE

Greek Rule Over Palestine 333-165   Palestine under the Ptolemies 323-198

Alexander the Great 336-323
Ptolemaic Dynasty of Egypt
Ptolemy I 323-283
Ptolemy II 283-246
Ptolemy III 246-221
Ptolemy IV 221-203
Ptolemy V 203-181

Isaiah 24-27
Proverbs
Song of Songs
Esther
Ecclesiastes

200 B.C.

BATTLE OF BANION 198
Palestine under Seleucids 198-168

Seleucid Dynasty of Syria
Antiochus III 223-187
Seleucis IV 183-175
Antiochus IV (Antiochus Epiphanes) 175-163
Hasmonean Kingdom 165-63

MACCABEAN REVOLT 168
Judas Maccabee 166-160
Jonathan 160-142
Simon 142-134
John Hyrcanus 134-104
Aristobulus 104-103

Daniel
Zechariah 9-14
End of Old Testament

100 B.C.

Christian Lamp

NEW TESTAMENT HISTORY

ROME

PALESTINE

Alexander Jannaeus 103-76 B.C.
Alexandra 76-67 B.C.
Aristobulus II 67-63 B.C.

Roman Rule Over Palestine 63 B.C.-A.D. 135
    POMPEY'S ENTRANCE INTO JERUSALEM 63 B.C.
    ASSASSINATION OF JULIUS CAESAR 44 B.C.
    BATTLE OF ACTIUM 31 B.C.
    Caesar Augustus 29 B.C.-A.D. 14

POMPEY'S ENTRANCE INTO JERUSALEM 63 B.C.
Hyrcanus II 63-40 B.C.
JERUSALEM TAKEN BY PARTHIANS 40 B.C.
Herod the Great 37-4 B.C.
BIRTH OF JESUS 6 B.C.
Archelaus 4 B.C.-A.D. 6

A.D.

Tiberius Caesar A.D. 14-37
MINISTRY OF JESUS A.D. 28-29
DEATH OF JESUS A.D. 29
MARTYRDOM OF STEPHEN AND
CONVERSION OF SAUL A.D. 35
Caligula A.D. 37-41
BARNABAS AND SAUL, ANTIOCH AND
JERUSALEM A.D. 41-42
PERSECUTION OF HEROD AGRIPPA I A.D. 44
PAUL'S FIRST JOURNEY, COUNCIL
AT JERUSALEM A.D. 46-47

Herod Antipas 4 B.C.-A.D. 34
Roman Procurators in Palestine 6 B.C.-A.D. 37
    Philip 4 B.C.-A.D. 37
    Pontius Pilate A.D. 27-37

A.D. 50

I-II *Thessalonians*
Galatians
I-II *Corinthians*
Romans, Philippians
Colossians, Philemon
Mark
I-II *Timothy*
Titus
Luke, Acts
Matthew, James
John, Hebrews
I *John*
Revelation
II-III *John*
I *Peter, Jude*

Claudius A.D. 41-54
PAUL'S SECOND JOURNEY A.D. 48-51

PAUL'S THIRD JOURNEY A.D. 52-57
Nero A.D. 54-68
IMPRISONMENT OF PAUL A.D. 57-62
PERSECUTION OF NERO A.D. 64
Galba, Otto, Vitellius A.D. 68-69
Vespasian, A.D. 69-79
Titus A.D. 79-81
Domitian A.D. 81-96
Nerva A.D. 96-98

JEWISH REVOLT A.D. 66-70
FALL OF JERUSALEM A.D. 70
DESTRUCTION OF THE TEMPLE A.D. 70

A.D. 100

II *Peter*
End of New Testament

Trajan 98-117
Hadrian 117-138
REVOLT OF BAR-COCHBA 132-135

A.D. 135

INDEX

ROME
TRES TABERNAE
PUTEOLI
NAPLES

ITALIA

First page of Paul's letter to the Romans, in Codex Alexandrinus

MACEDONIA
DYRRHACHIUM
PHILIPPI
AMPHIPOLIS
NEAPOLIS
THESSALONICA
APOLLONIA

BEROEA

ACHAIA

CORINTH
CENCHREAE
ATHENS

CRETE
LASA
CAUDA

(Mediterra

PAUL

Tiber River

Pamphilus
Priscilla
Jordanorum
Thrason
Maius
Valentinus
Bassilla
Agnes
Pamphilus
Felicitas
AURELIAN WALL
Nicomedes
Hippolytus
Viale Regina
Cyriaca
QUIRINAL
VIMINAL
ESQUILINE
Calepodius
Duo Felices
Processus
Martinianus
CAPITALINI
PALA-
TINE
CAELIAN
Pontianus
AVEN-
TINE
Peter and
Marcellinus
Campana
Marcus Marcellianus
Yaeger
Vibia
Praetextatus
Commodilla
Sebastian
Thecla
Domitilla
Lucina
Callistus
Via Appia
Generosa
Polimanti
Nunziatella

THE CATACOMBS OF ROME

PETER

THE WORLD OF
AND THE

ROMAN PROVINCES ....
OTHER REGIONS ....
TOWNS AND CITIES KNOWN
OTHER PLACES ....
MAIN ROUTES FOLLOWED

CYRENAICA